# I Survived the Enemy
# in the House

Shawnetta N. Murray

First Printing 2017
Published by: Shawnetta N. Murray
Editor: Erick Markley
Cover and Cover layout: Krystal Parker
Cover Photography: Virgil Murray Photography, LLC

ISBN: 978-0-692-99312-5

Shawn_nikole@yahoo.com

# TABLE OF CONTENTS

ACKNOWLEDGEMENTS.............................................. 6

FORWARD .......................................................... 7

INTRODUCTION .......................................... 11

1: A CHILD IS BORN.................................... 13

2: NORTHRIDGE........................................... 16

3: THE TIDES ALWAYS CHANGE .......................... 22

4: MONSTERS ARE REAL.............................. 25

5: HELLO, BLUE EYES ................................. 29

6: 1987-1988......................................... 33

7: SOMEONE TO TALK TO ......................... 38

8: THE LETTER .......................................... 45

9: WHAT HAPPENS IN THIS HOUSE, STAYS IN
THIS HOUSE .................................................... 51

10: I CAN MAKE YOU FAMOUS ............................ 61

11: BOY CRAZY...........................................74

12: UNPOPULAR POPULARITY................................88

13: HIM OR ME ..........................................95

14: BACK WHERE I STARTED ..............................101

15: COULD THIS BE LOVE................................126

16: WHY DID I COME BACK ..............................135

17: WHY DID I GET MARRIED.............................141

18: BE STILL AND KNOW THAT I AM GOD.....156

19: IT'S A NEW SEASON.................................168

20: IT WAS GOD ........................................171

"Before I formed you in the womb I knew you, before you were born I set you apart; I appointed you as a prophet to the nations."

Jeremiah 1:5 NIV

# ACKNOWLEDGEMENTS

All glory and thanks to God and my Lord and savior Jesus Christ. Thank you to my husband, Virgil, my sons, Jalen and Alijah. Thank you to my Mom, Grandma and Auntie. Thank you to both of my Grandfathers; and to my entire family for always believing in me, loving me, pushing me, and motivating me. Thank you to my niece, KLW; you are a survivor and I love you so much. Thank you to all my friends - my angels sent from heaven - that have become family and taken this journey with me. Thank you to G.U.I.Dance (past and present). Thank you to my church babies and my church family. Thank you to my Bishop for all you have done and been in my life. To anyone and everyone that has ever poured into me or supported me in any way, know that you have blessed my life tremendously and I am forever grateful for each, and every one of you. Anybody reading this I thank you and dedicate this book to you. I pray a special prayer of healing, deliverance, strength, courage and that this be a blessing over your life. I love you all beyond words.

# FORWARD

Some years after I was an adult I had a conversation with mother about experiences that I had growing up. Some of the things were shocking, surprising to her. There were revelations that caught her off guard and even caused her to tear up. It was during this conservation that I became very reflective about many events that had occurred, and their impact in my life now as an adult.

My mother was confronted with the realization that there were things that she couldn't protect me from even within our home and family. The sense of feeling powerless, as she heard about some of the traumatic things her child went through made my mother angry; and as I pen this reflection, I wonder if on some level she may have felt as though she failed me as parent? However, the conversation took an unexpected turn when I shared with my mother what my experience was being parented by her. I acknowledged that although she did the best she could, there were things that I did not receive. These things were not material, nor were they things one could gather later on in life. Upset, by what I had said I vividly recall saying to my mother "You can't tell me what my experience was being parented by you, you can't write the narrative of my own lived experience." There was a moment of radio silence, as my truth had been spoken. How could she respond? What could she say?

There is a saying that "the body keeps the score." This reference is related to trauma, and the events one may experience and how they interpret that traumatic experience. Traditionally, when we think of trauma we think about some major event, a car accident, 9/11, something that says "yeah, that was big, that was traumatic,". The reality is, trauma isn't always visible. Trauma does not always appear on the 11'oclock news, nor does it always make the public headlines. The truth is some traumas are silent reminders, that causes one to feel like a voiceless victim. Trauma is the child who went to school and was constantly called a negative name. Now that child is an adult and continues to go through life trying to prove to yourself and others that you're not the label someone placed upon you. Trauma, is knowing that you are no longer in that situation where you felt unsafe and a sense of helplessness, but when you close your eyes you are reliving the pain, you smell the reminders of that traumatic event. At its core for many, trauma is knowing that no one believes you when you tell your story, when you have the courage to reveal your truth. Trauma, is feeling as though you're locked in the silence of shame at the expenses of your peace of mind, all the while wondering if what happened really happened, and was it "my fault?" Throughout the years, I have come to know and understand as a Licensed Mental Health Professional that there are two types of grief; grieving for what you had and lost, versus grieving for what you never received and coming to terms with that. We don't have to assume that it will never be or that something is wrong with us because we do not have it. How do we deal with or approach the scar that is the traumatic event in a way that empowers us and no longer holds us hostage in our mind and emotions?

The book you are about read, boldly tells the story of one woman who found the courage to tell her story and live in her truth. It's a testimony of resilience, faith and the power of God's restorative love. Mrs. Murray eloquently shares not only how she survived "The Enemy in the House," but how she recovered her sense of self, and discovered the plan and purpose that God had for her life. This is not a book to be read, it's one to be experienced as I'm sure there are many others who too have survived various enemies in their own house.

Jackey J. Smith, LCSW, PsyD
Licensed Psychotherapist

## Introduction

Sunday morning service was coming to close, and my Pastor had just opened the Altar for prayer. The praise team was softly singing "God can heal, He can deliver, He can mend your brokenness…" It was my Sunday to serve on the choir side. I sat there looking at the altar fill up and watching the tear soaked faces of men and women crying out to God and allowing the Holy Spirit to have His way with them. I could feel some of them, as if I was tapping into their hurt places. I could see some of their struggles, almost as if they were being played on a screen in front of me. Some of these struggles were similar to mine. My mind began to go back over my life. God had healed, delivered, and mended so much. I had been a member at this church for twelve years, and had grown a lot in my spiritual walk. My Pastor was so instrumental in that because he had taught me and held me up through so much. I was off almost in a full day dream; I could barely hear the voices of the praise team anymore. I closed my eyes and began to worship and thank God for all of it. Then I was brought back to reality by my pastor's voice as he ministered to me; he said "You hear me Nikki? If I wasn't preaching to anybody else today I was preaching to you." "The molestation you survived, the suicide you survived, the divorce you survived, the betrayal you survived, and now it' s time to tell your story." "Write the book!" he said; "it will be the deciding factor between whether someone chooses to live or die." "You have to write it, someone's life depends on it."

## 1: A CHILD IS BORN

From the day I was born it seemed like something, or someone, was trying to take me out. The odds always seemed to be stacked against me in some way or another. Born to a teenage mom and a slightly older father - both of whom were from challenging upbringings and quite troubled as a result. My father was in and out of jail, a victim of molestation and abuse; while my mother battled very similar demons. Their relationship was extremely dysfunctional and volatile. Both of my grandmothers were, ultimately, single parents and both battled with addiction of some form. My mother was fresh out of high school and my father was either fresh out of, or on his way back to, being locked up. Yet here they were faced with the ultimate responsibility; a life that was solely dependent upon theirs: a baby girl, me.

As an infant, I bounced around from place to place with my mom. I lived pretty much all over the East Bay; either with my parents in East Oakland, my mom's friends, or with my maternal grandmother, whom I simply call grandma. At one point I slept in a dresser drawer because I didn't have a crib or a bassinet. Between my mom's partying friends, her volatile relationship with my father, and my very own grandma, who was struggling with alcohol addiction, my mother somehow still managed to keep me safe…..or so it seemed. I was quite a sickly child. Before I was even six months old I fell ill with a fever so high I had to be admitted to the NICU and have a spinal tap performed to figure out what was wrong with me. Then again at 18 months old I fell ill with a terrible inner ear infection and spiked a fever so high that I went into a full blown seizure and stopped breathing. I had to be rushed to the hospital where I was admitted. Not only did I have struggles with my physical health, but at the time, I was witnessing things that would later affect me mentally. The abuse I witnessed my mother endure at the hands of my father is something that no child should ever have to witness; something that was so traumatic that, to this very day, I can still vividly remember bits and pieces as though they're playing on a screen right in front of me. Once he had beaten her so bad that she had to be taken to the hospital. The beating was so severe that I didn't recognize my mother and feared her. She had stitches on her eye, forehead and hand; her jaw was also badly injured; she had bruises and swelling everywhere. She was literally crying tears of blood. I wouldn't even go up to her. I told my grandma that there was a monster in the room. She was so badly beaten that they called priest in to pray for her. That wasn't the only time he had beaten her. Well, my father didn't serve much time for his vicious assault on my mom, and was stalking and threatening her before police were even able to find him and arrest him. Fearing for her life, and now having a place to escape to, my mom decided to pack up and move us over four hundred miles away.

## 2: NORTHRIDGE

My mom knew this guy from high school, named V, and they had become close. He was there attending CSUN on a scholarship and offered to let us come and stay with him and his roommates. A two-bedroom apartment with college boys was hardly the ideal environment for a young single mother and her two-year-old little girl. It wasn't all bad at first though.

I have some fond memories from back then. The early 1980's represented such an electric and free-spirited time. From the music, to the fashion, to the lifestyles - everything was so colorful, vibrant and free. One of my fondest memories of this time is when mom's "friend" and his roommate would toss me back and forth across the living room like I was a toy. They would swing me by my hands and my feet, to where I was almost positioned like a kettle bell, back and forth several times before catapulting me across the room into each other's arms. I loved when they did that! I would laugh so hard, and would always want them to keep doing it; that feeling of your stomach dropping out and the breath momentarily leaving your body; it was such an adrenaline rush. It was scary, but the good kind of scary. It drove my mom nuts though; it absolutely scared the crap out of her every time. She didn't experience the same kind of adrenaline rush that I did, nor was she as entertained as they were. Seeing her baby girl being tossed to and fro like a football, it almost seemed to momentarily paralyze her with fear. She never put a stop to it though. They continued to play this game with me until V's roommate moved out.

 On the flip side to the fun and games, I also have some memories of waking up to adults having sex on the floor in my room. Of course, at the time I didn't know what it was, but it's an image forever etched into my memory. I have vivid memories of a grown man and woman sprawled out completely naked on the floor, as I crept past them to use the restroom in the middle of the night; it's still so crystal clear in my mind. My mind was so young, fragile, and impressionable; still very much in its molding stages, and these were the kinds of images molding it. As I said, not an ideal situation for a child, but what other life did I know? V began taking on a fatherly role with me. During this period while attending school, he was employed at a popular sandwich shop a couple of miles away from where we lived. V would walk me to my preschool, which was only a couple of blocks away from where he worked.

The cold presence of death would once again strike when I was four years old. My school had this giant see-saw pillow that all the children would fight over. We all wanted to play on it, sit on it, nap on it, flip it over, jump on it - all but share it with one another. Me, being one of the tiniest in the class, I rarely made it onto that pillow. Finally when my turn came around, I felt like my then favorite cartoon character, She-Ra, on the top of the mountain top. I extended my arm as though I was raising my sword high towards the sky as I had seen her do so many times before. I was untouchable, on top of the world…..until my classmate came up on top of the mountain with me and brazenly sent me tumbling down the mountain side. That's right, just bulldozed her way up there and sent me crashing down onto the hardwood floor, head first. My head split right open, all the way down to my skull, cracking it. I still remember my blood soaked green dress and being carried several miles away to the ER because we didn't have a car then. My mother literally held me in her arms as the doctors stitched me up while I kicked and screamed. It seemed like they put a million stitches in my head and that I could feel every single one. My head is still indented and tender in that spot, but there was no brain damage or other residual effects. I was ready to go outside to play the next day. Like the energizer bunny, I took another licking and kept on ticking.

There were so many great people that came through that apartment complex and it evolved from having a college dorm feel to a more family oriented complex. Some of those people my mom and I still have contact with today. There was this one girl in particular that I adored. She was a bit older than me and she wasn't like me or my mom. She was more like our roommate. She had a fairer complexion and silkier hair compared to mine. To me she looked a lot like my Barbie dolls. Despite how different we looked, she treated me like a little sister. Often times, she would care for me when my mom and her "friend" went out on the weekends with their friends. She lived there at the complex with her father who was like a grandfather or uncle figure to a few of us kids in the complex. We all called him papa. I loved to be around them. Their environment was much different than mine, even though they lived only several doors down from me. So close, yet it seemed like an entire world away. Papa had this fish tank with fish I'd never seen before in it. It was the coolest thing to me. It seemed to tower over me and I would stand in front of it for what felt like hours just watching those fish swim around. Sometimes he'd even place a pinch of fish food in my hands and then lift me up to drop it into the water. Then he'd hold me up there to watch the fish scurry to the top of the tank to get the food. Papa also had a dog named Shasta. I did not share the same fascination with Shasta as I did with the fish. Shasta seemed gigantic to me, like something straight out of 'The Neverending Story." His bark seemed to echo through my entire body and consume me with fear. He terrified me to my teeny tiny core. Papa usually kept him contained though. That is until the day Shasta became the reason I almost drowned for the first time. While playing in the courtyard of the complex, I heard that bark. It seemed to be getting closer, so I looked to see where it was coming from. Sure enough, it was Shasta barreling towards me. He was friendly, but at the same time, so intimidating to me. I only had two options, run towards him or away from him. I ran away and he chased me straight into the deep end of the swimming pool. I paddled my hands so hard and so fast. I was crying, screaming, and sinking; water filling my mouth, muzzling my screams, and burning my nose as I gasped for air while going under. I was coughing and my arms were getting tired, and my legs felt too heavy to move. I didn't know what to do, I couldn't swim. Everything I was doing was instinctive. I was in survival mode and didn't even realize it because I was drowning and didn't even know it. The harder I fought to stay above water, the more I was sinking. There goes that cold presence of death again. The pool sat directly in the middle of the complex and people were always hanging out, so someone was always watching. Even though it felt like an eternity, it didn't take long at all for someone to jump in and pull me out of the water as I was sinking to the bottom of seven feet. I didn't know God then, but looking back now I know He had his hands on me!

## 3: THE TIDES ALWAYS CHANGE

Yes, so many fond memories of people from all different walks of life. If reality TV was thing back then, that complex would've had its own show. Like any reality show, no matter how good things are going, the drama will always ensue. Things began to get a little sketchy in my life between the ages of four and five. Quite a few significant changes took place that year and not necessarily for the better. I no longer identified mom's friend as V, but as something much more significant to her, and as "daddy" to me. Daddy injured his knee in a pickup game of football. This injury would prove to be life-changing for us all. Daddy lost his ability to run, which was a monumental setback for him. Now, faced with the stress and the worry of working, maintaining a family and dealing with all of life's other issues without his coping mechanism - all while technically still growing up - he began eating compulsively and gaining weight. He and mom began arguing more, or maybe I just noticed it more. At the time, I didn't know what the arguments were about, but later I'd hear stories of infidelities and other forms of betrayal. He worked during the day and attended a vocational school at night and later became an audio engineer. One thing about daddy was his work ethic. It almost seemed like an addiction. He worked hard to provide for us, or so it seemed. My life didn't only begin changing at home, but outside the home as well. I started attending Kindergarten at Anderson Elementary School, where I experienced bullying and racism almost immediately. My Kindergarten teacher was a beautiful tall black woman with my same complexion. It was the first time I ever saw my skin color as beautiful; back then, Vanna White was my idea of beauty. My teacher always wore the nicest clothes, super high heels, and different colored pearls to match whatever she was wearing. I wanted to be just like her. Yes, my mom too was my same complexion, tall, and skinny, but I didn't see her the same way. Now, as an adult, I figure that because of what I had to witness with her and at the hands of her, that maybe I couldn't see her beauty. Whatever the case, my Kindergarten teacher would be one of the only people to be kind to me during my six years at that school. I learned the difference between black and white in the form of name calling, unfair treatment and by being cast aside by both staff and students. Why weren't these white people like the ones in my complex? Why didn't they love me like papa? Why did they say mean things to me, hit me, and make me cry? My friends at home didn't treat me like this. This "big girl school" wasn't what I had expected. I didn't want to be there anymore. My teacher and a couple of kids were the only ones nice to me. I wanted to go home….but wait did I really want to go home?

## 4: MONSTERS ARE REAL

The first day of summer 1986, my mom and daddy got married. It was a beautiful wedding in a rose garden back home in Oakland. My cousin (who was more like my sister, a twin sister at that) and I, were flower girls. Too young to understand what all was going on, I do remember quite a bit of tension and drama taking place that day. While getting ready, mom had on this beautiful floral print robe and rollers in her hair. Her face was made up like a movie star. I only saw her like this when she would go out dancing with friends. Today was different though, it was as if I was watching her transform into a princess. She was completely acting the part of Cinderella going to the ball; she seemed like she was fighting to smile. My cousin and I danced and twirled around in our dresses with our hair perfectly done, and our dress shoes that slid across my grandpa's cement basement floor like tap shoes. Even in the midst of my twirling and dancing, I observed the sour expressions on some of the adults' faces - particularly on my aunt's face. She was fussing and cussing about something; although she tried to do is discreetly, I picked up on it. Something wasn't right about this day. Nonetheless, mom came out looking ready to go meet her Prince Charming at the ball. Late as could be, we all piled into the Limo and I couldn't take my eyes off that beautiful white dress. It was the most beautiful dress I'd ever laid eyes on. I wanted one just like it; maybe she would let me wear that one. I wanted to look like a queen too, not like the "nigger" the mean kids at school said I was. Oh, if they could see me now in this dress, with my shoes, they'd all want to be my friend and be nice because I looked like a beautiful princess. I wouldn't be hit or pushed, or called mean names in this dress. No one would be making me cry in this dress. I wouldn't feel alone or cast aside in this dress. I wanted to stay in this dress forever.

After saying "I do" to my mom, daddy began acting as though he owned my mom and I. He began "disciplining" me more and wanting total control. He became meaner to both my mom and I. The yelling seemed to be louder, the hitting seemed harder, and it felt like I would get beaten for any given reason. He had this belt that belonged to his late father. It looked like something you'd sharpen a razor with in a barbershop.

It was a thick and wide belt with a three-pronged buckle on it. It was as though he had set out to rule the house with fear and torment. Well, he did exactly that. I lived in absolute fear of him a majority of the time then. If he wasn't beating me, he was beating my mom or both of us at the same time. He was a ticking time bomb and his anger couldn't be controlled. We constantly walked on egg shells around him. My first time being beaten with that belt - I can't remember the reason why I was in trouble - but I'll never forget that pain. The bass in his voice always seemed to make my heart stop. It was like I recognized the evil in his voice before I even really knew what evil was. He screamed my name, "Nikole!" and snatched me up by one arm. Cussing and spit flying from his mouth as he dangled me by one arm while shaking me like a ragdoll. He would fling me into the room and yell "drop em!" He proceeded to beat me with that belt while I was completely naked from the waist down. I was left with broken and bleeding skin. Welts all up and down my behind, legs, back, and arms from trying to defend myself. I was left in that room crying and while my body felt like it was on fire. Every movement I made hurt. I was hurt, confused and with my little spirit broken and consumed with fear. I wondered: would he come back? Where was my mommy? What had I done to deserve that? Somehow, I knew it was all too excessive. The thing that stuck out the most in my mind was the fact that I had to take my pants off. Somehow, I knew it wasn't right, but the look on his face as he watched and snapped that belt, while I slowly pulled my pants and underwear off, burns in my mind. The eyes I was looking into and the pleasure on his face as he watched the terror and confusion in my eyes were like none I had looked into before. This was different, but this was discipline as normal. My first memories of daddy inappropriately touching me began around this time. Those moments of violation were always masked with tickling and rough-house play. As I look back, it was like we had entered a new realm of some sort. In this realm, those beatings, and worse, became common place. In this realm, something very bad had been unleashed. Something I would become all too familiar with. Shawnetta, meet the monster in the house..

## 5: HELLO, BLUE EYES

When I was 6, I met a little white girl that lived in the apartment complex next to ours. She had piercing blue eyes. I remember wishing I had eyes like hers. We played together almost every day. Her and I lived so close to each other, that we'd be able to take a very short walk down the alley, from one gate to the next, to get to each other's apartment complex to play. Her parents always allowed her to come over and play with us. Blue-eyes was a few years older than me and extremely bossy. She wasn't mean to me like the other white kids I went to school with, so I still played with her. She always wanted to play house and always wanted to play husband and wife. It wasn't a big deal at first, but then she started wanting to pretend kiss. Something inside me knew I shouldn't be pretending to kiss, or even really kissing girls. I just wasn't comfortable with it, but if I refused, she wouldn't play with me anymore. So I went along with it. One day while playing in my room, we set up, what we called a fortress. We hung my strawberry shortcake sheets and blankets from one side of my bed to one side of my dresser; and anchored them with several of my encyclopedias. We got underneath the canopy we made and began playing. Blue-eyes wanted to play house again. We sat across from each other Indian style and she would say "Nikki, cover your mouth with your hand like this" as she covered her mouth with the palm of her hand. I did the same and she leaned in and our hands touched. I remember thinking that it wasn't as bad as I thought. That didn't last long though. She then instructed me to lie down, and she climbed on top of me and continued to pretend kiss. I didn't want to play anymore. Daddy was in the next room, what if he came in? He'd beat me for sure. He'd beat us both. Blue-eyes was so insistent, and I wanted her to still be my friend, so I didn't stop her. She then said "Nikki kiss me down here." I was so confused and I told her that we weren't supposed to be doing this. I don't know how I knew, but I knew. I wasn't supposed to touch her private area, let alone kiss it. She managed to convince me to let her show me how, and it wasn't long before she took my pants down began kissing me down there. It was a strange feeling and I wasn't sure why I couldn't, or didn't want to, make her stop. Eventually she did stop though, and then asked me to do the same to her. After a few minutes of convincing, I did it too. Then, finally, I told her I didn't like this game and that I wanted to play Barbies instead. She decided she wanted to go home. We never played together again after that. I didn't think of that day for many years to come.

A new girl, named Jae, and her mom moved into the corner apartment a few doors down from me. We became instant friends. She was so nice to me, unlike the other white kids at school; and she didn't want to play house like Blue-eyes. I would go Jae to visit her grandparents and would spend a lot of time at her apartment. She seemed to have it all. Often I would imagine her life was mine, to escape the reality of my actual life. Yes, I had every Barbie and toy you could imagine as well as clothes galore, and the latest high-tech gadgets. She did too, but hers always seemed better than mine because hers didn't come with the price tag of beatings like mine seemed to. I almost always got the toys and things I asked for. However, it was as if I received those things to make up for the abuse I endured. The abuse I thought I was hiding well. One day while playing at her apartment her mom came to me and asked "Nikki, are you being mistreated at home?" The thought of what would happen to me if I told her the truth, frightened me almost half to death, so I lied and said "no." She never asked me again.

## 6: 1987-1988

When I was seven years old there seemed to be a ray of sunshine peaking through the dark cloud that was my life. I was going to be a big sister! I wanted a little sister so bad, but my mom was convinced it was a boy. Months before my younger sibling made a debut, my world came crashing down. I was outside playing and one of our neighbors came outside crying a very loud painful cry. Then like wildfire the news spread: while visiting her mom in Arizona, my friend that was like a big sister to me, was in a car accident and got ejected and died. Only 16 years old and she was gone. That was a rough summer for me. I'd never lost anyone before, and I thought people only died from old age. I remember feeling like anyone around me, old or young, could die at any moment. That thought terrified me and I cried most of the time because of it. I don't recall too much abuse during that time. Maybe it was because my mom was with child and was his first and only biological child. That was also around the time I began to feel the difference between biological child and step-child. I was their daughter in front of people, but only mommy's daughter in private. Third grade came and I was eight years old. I was on cloud nine, because it was almost time for my baby sibling to make his or her debut. The bullying didn't seem to faze me the same way anymore. I met the only other person at my Elementary school that was nice to me. My third grade teacher, another black woman. Not as pretty as my Kindergarten teacher, but so very nice all the same. She would be the one to challenge me to take a step I had never taken before. Finally, my younger brother was here! I couldn't have been more excited and in awe. I just loved him so much. I remember holding him for the first time and asking my mom why he smelled the way he did. I loved the way he smelled (that newborn smell); I loved every single thing about him. He was my baby brother and I told myself that I was going to protect him with every ounce of my being. Well, it didn't take daddy long to start showing preferential treatment, and it wasn't long before he zoned in on me again. It didn't faze me much at first because I was so excited about my baby brother. My mom would walk to school with him in the stroller to pick me up and I wanted the world to see him. One day after school my teacher asked me to stay after class for a moment to speak with her. She began asking me questions about home and a bruise on my arm. She told me that she noticed multiple bruises on me several times before, and that my demeanor at times made her feel like something was happening at home. She flat out asked me if I knew what molestation was and if I had ever been molested. I felt so safe with her, unlike with anyone else before, and I let my guard down. I let it all spill out. It was like I couldn't stop. The flood gates had opened up. I told her about the beatings and the inappropriate touching and "tickling." I told her how he hit my mom and how he fought my aunt. I also told her about how out of control his temper was. I told that woman everything. It didn't take any amount of time for me to wish I hadn't mumbled a single word. Before I knew it, I was in the principal's office with the police and a woman that said she was with an agency to protect children like me. I was horrified. When my mom got to the school to pick me up, they wouldn't let her see me. Then he showed up. I knew it was over for me then. What did I do? Why did I say anything at all? I'm going to get it. I want my mommy! That lady and those officers asked me a ton of questions in a million different ways. The more they asked, and the more I had to repeat what I told my teacher, the more scared I became. I just kept asking for my mom and crying. Finally, they let my mom in, but she didn't come without him. He was being so nice, it was weird and I didn't know what to make of his behavior. He was too calm and it kind of scared me. He proceeded to ask me questions like "why didn't I tell him I didn't like when he tickled me?" and saying things like "we're just rough housing when I hit you, it's not to hurt you." and "I would never hurt you or your mom, I love you." I was so confused. I started to doubt what I knew to be true and wrong. What he had been doing was wrong. I remember thinking to myself "mommy, say something, tell them he hits you too." She never told on him. Instead, he and my mom started telling me that because of what I said the people were going to take me away. They told me that if I didn't say it wasn't true that I was going to have to live with a family that I didn't know and that I wouldn't have any of my things, my toys, or my clothes anymore. What did it for me was when they told me that I would never get to see my mommy, grandma, aunt, or my baby brother again. No,

I could never go without my baby brother. In that moment I remember feeling defeated, absolutely defeated and alone. Then, just like that, I recanted my entire story. I got to go home with them and he didn't unleash his fury on me right away. Matter of fact, it was several weeks before I would feel his wrath again.

## 7: SOMEONE TO TALK TO

Child protective services did investigate and follow up with us for about a year. They ordered us into therapy. Daddy was less than thrilled about it. Once a week I had to go sit in this strange, but nice, white lady's office. It wasn't a very big office, but it had a desk, a couch, a bookcase, and lots of dolls and stuffed animals. I was more excited about the toys than anything. Maybe my focus was on the toys because I didn't know what to expect from the lady. I was completely sure why I was there at first. I wasn't completely sure why I was there at first. She would ask me all kinds of questions about home and him. She would use Barbies and dolls to try to get me to act out our interactions at home. In the beginning, I didn't say a word and I would just play with the dolls. Occasionally, I'd mention my brother, or even the horrible people at school. I knew better than to say anything bad about daddy though. This lady was good though and somehow she broke down the barrier I had up. I started to tell her little bits and pieces. After every one of our sessions she would have me wait in the waiting room, while he and my mom went in to speak with her. One day after she spoke with them, I knew she had repeated some of what I said. The look on his face when he came out of her office let me know that it wasn't going to be a good night for me. Mommy and daddy drove separate cars to our session that day, so I rode home with my mom. I just needed a few more moments of some sort of peace before the wrath ensued. It helped me to feel a little better. Once we got home and I could see that he was there, every bit of fear set in. There I was right back in hell again; another day, another beating. I remember thinking that I'd never open my mouth again. As I got older the beatings got worse. I began to go through puberty way before any of my peers, and this made my days at school much worse. I felt like a mutant and was treated as such by my classmates. At home though, I was getting a different kind of attention from him; a different level of interest in me surfaced. An interest I was far from fond of. This was the phase of my life where my feelings of self-hate emerged. Fifth grade would prove to be one of the most difficult years of my adolescence. My body was developing and I was the only one of my friends that had breasts and that had started my cycle. My mom, grandma, and Aunt threw me a little period party. They prepared a menstrual cycle kit. It contained pads, body spray, Midol, candy, and snacks in it. Then we ordered pizza, popped popcorn, and watched movies; just the four of us. They had gotten the idea from an episode of "The Bill Cosby Show", where Rudy started her cycle. Truly, this was one of my fondest memories from this time in my life. They turned something that was so embarrassing and seemingly abnormal for my age, into a moment I would cherish forever. The rest of the time though, I was constantly hiding myself to avoid being teased - as if the kids at school needed anything else to make fun of me about. This insecurity with my body stayed with me well into my adult life. So many physical and emotional changes were occurring and I was feeling even more alone and isolated than ever, like even more of an outsider. Daddy sensed it, and he prayed on it. One day I came home from school and he sat me down and said we needed to talk. He began the conversation by acknowledging the changes my body was going through, and how "strange" I had been acting with him. I remember thinking that I just didn't want him anywhere near me. He then went on to say how he noticed I only wanted to play with girls. I sat there and thought to myself that I am a little girl, I'm supposed to play with little girls; and boys are mean. "I am a little girl. He then made a reference to our neighbors, a lesbian couple. At the time I wasn't sure of the meaning lesbian, but what I did know was that two women lived next door and kissed each other in ways that husbands and wives kiss each other. Then the memory blue-eyes and the things she did to me that day came to me. I was so afraid and felt so much shame. Not fully understanding what I experienced with her, but in some way, I knew it was wrong. Was that what our neighbors do? Did he know about blue-eyes? Did he see us? Will he tell my mom? Where was he going with this? Daddy looked me in my eyes, as his lips curled into a slight smirk, then said to me "Nikki, you're like them, you're gay." I didn't say anything at first, I just stared at him confused. He then said to me "you like girls, Nikki, and that is disgusting, but it's who you are." He told me that people hate gay people and that bad things will happen to me because I was gay. I will never forget hearing those words and the instantaneous disgust I felt. Was it true? I liked a boy at school though. I've never wanted

41

to kiss a girl. She made me do it. Am I disgusting? Will people hate me more than they already do? He said he was going to help me change that though. Help me how? I then told him about the boy I liked and denied his accusations. I told him I didn't need help changing anything. Daddy became frustrated with me and called me a liar. He told me his father had the same talk with him when he was in the fifth grade, and that he helped him. Helped him how? I didn't need help though; what was going on here? Why was daddy saying these things to me? Where was my mommy? After some time of drilling me and reducing me to tears and shame, he sent me off to my room. He told me not to tell my mom or he'd beat me and put me on restriction. So I said nothing to her about it. That conversation changed me though and I didn't want to be around anybody after that. I didn't want to go outside and play. I felt gross and was afraid that other people would think what he thought. That was the beginning of the many mind games he would play with me throughout my upbringing. School became more difficult. I had an extremely racist teacher in the fifth grade and the bullying became more relentless. The whites didn't like me because I was black. The blacks and Hispanics that got bussed in from Los Angeles, didn't like me because I lived in a better part of town and "talked white." I couldn't tell on any of them because it would make the situation worse. One weekend while at my grandma's, I told my aunt about this one girl, named Dani, from Los Angeles. Dani would follow me around the playground with her friends hitting and pushing me. I was so afraid of her. Actually, I was afraid of everyone. Fear was all I knew. Fear was all I had ever learned in my life. My Aunt caught the bus up to my school that following week and made me fight her. She would've made me fight anyone that was bullying me, but because I told her specifically about Dani; that was who my Aunt felt needed to made an example of. My aunt being there gave me a new feeling, an unfamiliar feeling: courage. I had never stood up to my bullies before, but my Aunt believed I could defend myself against Dani. My aunt coached me through that entire altercation in the girl's bathroom. I let all of my frustration out on Dani. I left her in the bathroom crying and with the contents of her backpack emptied into the toilet. From that day forward, she never bothered me again. I never tolerated bullying from anyone else at school.

## 8: THE LETTER

This "courage" got me into a bit of trouble in class one day though. I sassed off to my teacher. After all, she was a bit of a bully too. She didn't take too kindly to this new attitude and let me know she'd be calling my parents after school. Immediately the courage was replaced with the all too familiar feeling of fear. I knew exactly what would happen if she called my house. I began to cry hysterically. Hot salty tears soaked my face as I apologized and begged her not to call. She was not having it though. That was the longest walk home ever. I steered clear of him when I got home. I went straight to my room to do my homework. I didn't even play with my toys or ask to go outside that day. I was in the bathroom when it happened. The phone rang and it was as if the ring was louder than normal, alerting me that it was her calling. I heard daddy answer the phone and I was so scared. I didn't know what to do, so I locked the bathroom door. "Nikole!" he shouted. The echo of my name seemed to bounce off of every wall in the entire complex. I cowered between the toilet and the bathtub with the plunger in my hand. I knew good and well that wouldn't save me though. The door handle was jiggling as he tried to get in. The bathroom door crashed open with the sound of wood cracking. "You want to act up in class and fucking embarrass me? I'll kill you, you little bitch!" his voice was booming. I couldn't move. Why did I hide here?! Why didn't I run out of the apartment?! Why did I come home?! Mommy! He slapped me so hard that I flew out of the corner I was in to the adjacent corner of the bathroom; my tiny frame slamming into part of the bathtub. He just kept slapping me, yelling, and spit was flying everywhere. Then he wrapped his hands around my throat and began strangling me. Hard as I tried, I could not break his hold. I couldn't breathe. Why wasn't anyone here to save me? I wanted my mommy more than anything in that moment. Then everything went dark and quiet for what seemed like an eternity. I don't know how long I was out, but I came to with him shaking me and calling my name "Nikki, Nikki." He seemed a little shaken up; the fury that was once in his eyes had disappeared. He was scared; he'd thought he'd really done it this time. Hell, I thought so too. Not a word was mentioned to my mother about the phone call or the beating. If he did mention it to her, she didn't say anything to me. She did notice the door though. I remember daddy making some excuse about why he had to bust it open. That night I cried and wrote. I didn't want to live anymore. Between the bullying I endured at school and the abuse I endured at home, I just wanted to die. I wasn't sure where people went when they died, but I figured it had to be better than being here. Better than being in a place where everyone hates you. He hated me, the kids at school hated me, my teacher hated me; I figured only the special needs kids I volunteered with liked me, but I figured that only because they didn't have the mental capacity to hate me or anyone else. As I wrote I could hear the kids taunting me with things like "Nikki picky lick my dicky" or "you think you're white, you're just an ugly black girl that talks funny." I could hear daddy telling me that I was gay and how disgusting I was. My pain just spilled out onto the pages as I wrote and cried. I reflected on the good times like our Thursday family nights, the awesome birthdays and Christmases, but it made it hurt worse. I was so confused and mixed up emotionally. I felt so alone, so unloved, and so unaccepted. This would be the first, but definitely not the last time, I planned to run away. Here I was at nine years old, wanting to run away from home. Nobody wanted me around anyway. It seemed as if they'd all be happier if I weren't around, or if I hurt myself. I started to imagine ways I would do it. Then in vivid detail I wrote down how I would slit my wrist in the classroom in front of my teacher, the horrible bullies, and him. I wrote down how they would watch me bleed out and how happy they would be to see me die because they hated me so much. That letter was probably the most disturbing thing I had ever written;. so much pain and torment. I just went on and on. When I was done writing, something else came over me. The belt! I had to grab that God-awful belt and get rid of it. I don't know where this courage came from, but I liked it. I felt alive and fearless. I decided to take the trash out. As I walked down the alley to the giant green dumpster, I temporarily lost my sense of courage. My palms began sweating and my heart raced. I kept looking over my shoulder thinking someone might see me, or worse, that he might see me. Here I was standing in front of the dumpster doubting the decision I was about to make. I wanted to take away his power and ability to hurt me. I wanted to put an end to it. This belt, his weapon of choice, had to go. Without further hesitation, I took a deep breath, plopped it at the top of the trash can I was holding, and tossed the entire contents over into the dumpster. Just like that the belt was gone and he would be pissed when he found out. I didn't care though, because while writing that letter I had already made up in my mind that that would be the last night anyone would ever see me again. I was leaving this place! I decided not to try to do anything to myself at school because someone would stop me; besides, I wasn't sure I wanted to harm myself. I did, however, give my teacher that letter. The bell rang and there was a lot of chatter from the students settling in to their desks, yet I heard nothing about it. I blocked out everything around me as I zoned in on her reading that letter. Sheer horror came over her face as she read it and I watched. My plan failed though and that letter got me kicked out of school and the school district. I was on a sort of suicide watch, or very close monitoring, at home too because of it. I even had to go to daycare with my little brother every day, while mommy and daddy went to work. The school allowed me to finish the year out on home study.

Some good came out of that plan though because he was actually being nice to me. He was strangely happy. They purchased a home and we were moving. I was finally getting away….well, not from everybody.

## 9: WHAT HAPPENS IN THIS HOUSE, STAYS IN THIS HOUSE

In 1990, we relocated to a city that seemed a million miles away from Northridge. Even though Palmdale was only about an hour away from Northridge, I felt as though I was in another state. The San Fernando Valley and the Antelope Valley seemed worlds apart to me. Unlike most children my age, I wasn't sad about the move. I was actually elated because this would be a fresh start. A three-bedroom and two bathroom house with a huge back and front yard. Finally, my own room! Daddy and my mom were so over the moon. To be black and not even be thirty years old owners of a beautiful home there in Palmdale. That was almost unheard of. The new motto though was "we have no money." This motto at first was very light-hearted and made us laugh every time they said it. Later down the road, the stresses that the statement was based on would provoke more anger and frustration, which would lead to more abuse. In the meantime, I loved that place and was making friends, one of the first was a girl named Jessilyn. I started the sixth grade at

Ocotillo Elementary. Here, I had friends - a lot of them! People liked me, I was popular, and I certainly wasn't bullied. Well, except for one girl named Charleigh, whom I didn't much care for at first. Charleigh was the tallest girl in the sixth grade, and she was a tad bit bossy. Being bullied at my previous school gave me need to overcompensate for my short stature. Therefore, I wasn't about to let Charleigh think she could intimidate me with her height. I took every opportunity to let her know that she didn't scare me. Which caused her to think that I thought I was better than her. Little did I know, that wasn't at all what she was doing. We soon discovered that were so wrong about each other, and she would wind up being one of my closest friends, like a sister. I would come to gain a few "sisters" along the way. While at school one day, which was predominantly white, a new girl appeared. Yes, I was no longer the "new kid" and people liked me, so I introduced myself. I walked up to this skinny, lanky girl with a butterscotch complexion and simply said "Hi, my name is Nikki." Her name was Lynae and we hit it off immediately. Once we found out that we lived around the corner from each other, we became practically inseparable. We haven't missed a moment of each other's lives since. Out of the other two of my friends, Jessilyn and Charleigh, Lynae witnessed the most; not just the abuse towards me, but also towards my mom, and the favoritism shown towards my brother. She got, at the very least, a glimpse of everything. Yet as much as she witnessed, still so much was hidden from even her eyes. Lynae's house was my escape and her mom and step-dad embraced me as if I was one of their own. Her entire family did. Her mom, Hazel, would be yet another person to ask me if I was being abused at home. Why were people always asking me this? I, along with mommy and my little brother, were so conditioned to hiding the abuse that my mom and I endured in our home; at the hands of daddy. Was I not good at hiding it? The front we put on for everyone around us, because he made us, she saw right through it. I denied it for years to come, but she knew, she always knew. She was like my second mom and still is to this day. My friends never really liked to come over to my house. They all loved my mom and my baby brother, but nobody ever felt comfortable around daddy. Two of the most common words to describe him were "mean" and "creepy." One of my friends, named Carrie wasn't as intimidated by him, and loved nothing more than to just get away from her own house. She was being raised by just her father and she had two brothers as well. They were extremely racist. For some reason her father said it was ok for her to play with me. Daddy allowed me to stay the night at her house and she at mine. Her father would be the first adult I'd ever hear use the word "nigger" when referring to black people. I thought only the mean kids at school talked like that. It never registered that adults talked like that too. He took a strange interest in me, and being at her house had a peculiar vibe, a familiar one; kind of like home. I treaded lightly over there. One weekend, she came to stay the night at my house. We stayed up all night playing Sega and watching movies on USA, movies we had no business watching at ten years old. I was allowed to watch things like that though. Being exposed to things inappropriate for my age was common place in my house. We literally watched the sun rise that morning, so when he woke us up to clean just a few short hours later, we were less than pleased. "Nikole!" he shouted "Come eat, so we can get to this yard!" I remember dragging into the kitchen with her trailing closely behind me. He was standing there with plates in his hand. The air filled with the sweet and salty aroma of maple bacon, along with the fresh garden smell from the chopped onion and mushrooms my mom put in the scrambled eggs, and coffee too. We had these shiny black, ceramic, octagon shaped dinner plates. I reached out my hand to grab a plate from him and "Whaaaap!!" My right ear started ringing and my face went numb. Tears began streaming down and I didn't know if it was from crying or the impact of the plate across my face making my eyes water. He smacked me with the plate, and hard! I was frozen; I literally could not take a step forward or backward. I couldn't even lift my hand to touch my face. I was frozen with fear! He didn't care that I had company either. This really scared me: him not putting on a façade for people scared me something fierce. Times like that, you knew he was liable to do anything. He was in full on "not giving a single care" mode. I stood there as he yelled "Don't you ever walk into a room I'm in and not greet me, you little ungrateful bitch!" Mommy didn't come to my rescue. I had to pull myself together and went on as if nothing was wrong. Even though we remained friends for a few more years, Carrie never came to my house again after that. We still hung out at school and I still stayed over at her house sometimes. I walked in the bathroom one day at school and she was in a stall crying. I knew her voice and could see the shoes she had on underneath. She opened the door and her face was soaked with tears and beet red. She had an object in her hand, but was hiding it. After a minute or two, I convinced her to show it to me. It was a broken piece of a spork from lunchtime and her wrist was as red as her face. She had what seemed like a million scratches; some bleeding and some scabbed up already. She was trying to slit her wrist - eleven years old and wanting to leave this earth. Was her life at home that bad, and had I truly sensed that familiar vibe in her home? I was worried, but at the same time, strangely intrigued. "Could I do this too?" I thought. I made her throw the plastic away and we went to the nurse's office to get her some band-aids. We told the nurse that she fell and scraped up her arm. That night at home, while listening to them scream and fight in their room, I imagined slitting my own wrist like I'd seen in the movies. I had no clue of what was on the other side, or if there was one, but I was certain that anything had to be better than this. Dying seemed amazing to me, even though I hadn't truly grasped what exactly it meant to die. I wouldn't attempt it that night, but soon, real soon I would. My obsession with "a way out" was growing rapidly, and I was becoming more and more agitated. My home was in absolute chaos. My writing didn't sooth me as it had done before. Daddy was beating one of us just about every day. Mommy and daddy's friends even had to come over and break up the fights. There were holes in the walls, doors broken off the hinges, broken glass, and missing tiles on the kitchen counter from someone being slammed into it; all left evidence of the monster that raged within daddy. Yet we had to suck it up and put on our "happy family" mask as we ventured out into the world on a daily basis. I wasn't going to my therapy sessions anymore now that we lived so far away. All my fear, all of my hurt, all of my confusion, all of my depression was boiling over inside of me. One day I had reached my breaking point. I was walking down the street with Lynae and Jessilyn, and they were being so silly and goofy. I just wasn't in the mood. "What's wrong with you?" one of them asked. I replied "Nothing!" as I spewed off foul names and curse words at the two of them. They didn't like that at all, and they made sure to let me know. Then I stormed off, heading back home. Why had I just said that to them? They didn't deserve that, but I was too embarrassed by my outburst to apologize. That kind of verbal abuse was all I knew; that was the only way I knew how to express my frustration and hurt. I learned at a very young age how to cut people with my words. My mouth had already become so foul, and only got worse as I got older. I eventually reached a point where I almost enjoyed cussing people out, and being abusive with my words. A product of my environment, a product of daddy. Neither Lynae or Jessilyn spoke to me for what seemed like an eternity. Might've been only about a month, but it was long enough to break me.

I was home alone for a few hours one day and I got a steak knife out of the kitchen. I got in the tub because clearly I had watched too many depictions on TV and began scratching. Lightly at first, as if to just taunt myself, then I began applying more pressure. Just as I almost fully committed to doing this, I screamed "OUCH!" then blood appeared and started running down my arm. This hurt a bit more than I expected, but I kind of enjoyed it though. – it was almost like a release. Then the car alarm chirped indicating that he was home. I went into sheer panic mode. He would beat me so bad if he knew. Not because I was trying to take my life, but because I was getting blood everywhere. I threw the knife in the dishwasher and raced back into my room, jumped in my bed and pretended to sleep. My secret was safe for now.

The school year ended, and summer came. I had my friends back: the Three Musketeers, as my mom called us, were back into effect. A movie called Boyz n the Hood was in theaters and my love for gangster rap and alternative music was in full effect. The pain, sadness, and anger in these genres spoke to me in a way I couldn't quite describe. Those lyrics over a nice beat or sounds of a rock guitar somehow comforted me and fueled every negative feeling in me at the same time. Cross Colours were the current trend and my music of choice was blasting through my Walkman headphones. I was spending time with my family in Oakland as we were back and forth there a lot - after all, it was home. Well, some of the chaos in the house had simmered down a bit, or maybe I was having such a great summer that I tuned it out.

## 10: I CAN MAKE YOU FAMOUS

Mom and I took a trip to Oakland. This trip was a little different though. Mommy was acting a little strange. She was up to something. Were we finally leaving? I didn't get to say goodbye to my friends. I didn't grab all of my things. Why was she being so strange? While visiting my grandpa John and grandma Datha, my mom tells me someone was waiting outside to see me. Was it one of my cousins? Or was it my favorite Uncle Juron? She wouldn't tell me, she just insisted I come outside. There he was, my own face looking back at me. Anybody that said I was my mom's twin, clearly had never seen him before. He was a complete stranger to me, yet not a stranger at all. He hugged me so tight. My mom was very uneasy though, and the two had some exchanges that I couldn't tell if they were joking or serious. She never let him too close to her though. He had a pair of purple suede L.A. Gear lowtop sneakers for me. I was so excited! He thought it was because of the shoes. That wasn't it though; I was excited to have my biological father; my real dad! No more could daddy hurt me because my real dad was here, and he had the biggest arms I'd ever seen. My mommy didn't save me, but I just knew my real dad would. Daddy wouldn't want any part of him; my real dad looked as if he could crush every bone in daddy's body. He wasn't very tall, but his muscles were gigantic. We walked a couple of blocks down to a small complex of about four to six units, and I got to meet one of my uncles. He was just as built as real dad; man, I have a real dad I thought to myself. He was going to pick me up for holidays and take me on trips, and rescue me from my hell. He was going to be a father to me, more of a "daddy" than daddy had ever been. Later that night, my mom, auntie Andreya, and I drove out to a city called Fairfield. To my surprise, it was to see him again. He had a house that was about the same size as ours. He introduced us to his wife, a white woman, and his three step-daughters whom were also white. The oldest one was the same age as me, and her younger sisters were a set of twins. They were all so beautiful to me. The twins were so adorable; one had blonde hair and blue eyes, while the other was brunette with brown eyes, yet they looked the same. The older sister had an all too familiar disposition and an energy I knew way too well; a role I had seen played too many times before. Was I looking at myself? I felt it, yet I ignored it. I was having so much fun. I didn't want to leave! Then they brought in another surprise: a puppy!! The puppy had the markings of a Rottweiler, but the long fluffy coat of a Chow. I was on cloud nine. We talked, we played, we ate, and we laughed. Then it happened, he asked me about him. He asked how he treated me and how he treated my mom. He told me if he ever did anything to hurt us, he would make sure he was taken care of. I didn't know exactly what he meant by that, but it shook me a bit, and I knew not to dare tell him what I was going through. We left and I heard from him only one time after that. I never got any of the letters he promised; he never came to visit; he never sent for me. I was back in hell and it seemed as though Satan turned the heat up a notch. I didn't know what it was at the time, but I gravitated to this Bible I found. I never really opened it, but when things were in an uproar, I kept it close. When I felt fear for any reason, I'd grab my Bible as soon as I could get to it. Strangely, it helped to calm me and erase my fear, even if only for a moment. It was as if, even though I hadn't read the contents of it, I somehow knew that what was inside of it had the power to keep me safe. Soon I'd meet another protector of mine.

We took a trip to see one of my mom's clients from the law firm. Mom, my brother, daddy and I were lead into this tiny bathroom in the back of her client's house. I didn't know why we were there. There wasn't any food or drinks served, so it wasn't a party. Yet, there were several other people there as well. When they opened the door, my heart flipped and I squealed with joy. Puppies! A room full of beautiful little Rottweiler puppies. My brother and I almost couldn't contain our excitement as we played with them. Mom said we could pick one. We were getting a dog! I always wanted a dog, but I wasn't sure I believed he was going to let us have one. They were all jumping and running around us as we tried to decide which one we wanted to take home. All were running around except for one female puppy. As I sat on the edge of the tub petting the active puppies, one calmly came over to me and put her paw on my leg as if to signal me to pick her up. I picked her up and sat her in my lap and she immediately curled up into a ball and fell asleep and I fell in love. "Mommy, she picked me, this is the one; this is our puppy." We named her Maxi and she wouldn't come home with us for several more weeks, but when she did we became almost inseparable. She protected me when she could on many occasions. Always stood up for me and tried to defend me from his abuse in her own special way. Most times daddy would just kick and hit her too. Man's best friend, my best friend. That she would be for sixteen years.

My twelfth birthday was approaching, and as my body filled out more, I began admiring and aspiring to be a model, like the ones in the lingerie catalogs my mom would get. Daddy would encourage me, whenever I would talk about being a model like them. It gave me a sense of approval from him, which was something I rarely felt, yet needed. It was like a false sense of a healthy father and daughter relationship. Then one day he came to me and tells me he entered me into a modeling competition in Europe. He told me if I won that I would get a modeling contract and be able to be a model like the women in the catalogs my mom had. He told me I had to be thirteen though, so if anyone asked to lie and tell them I was. After all, I could pass for sixteen built the way I was. He took me to the mall and got me a new pair of Cross Colour jeans and a bodysuit. I couldn't believe he was letting me get a bodysuit. He said that I needed to dress a little older for them to believe that I was. One day he calls and tells me not to go outside and play and to be there when he got home from work. He worked swing shift and my mom worked a nine to five. We spent a lot of time alone in that house, him and I. He used that to his advantage. He gets home and tells me we have to submit our first video for the competition. This baffled me because I thought models took pictures and walked down runways. Why were we making a video? He made me change into the outfit he bought me from the mall and he put on some music. The song playing was "Here we Go Again" by a group named Portrait. He told me to dance around, "sexy like." I had no clue what sexy was. He wanted me to dance like the women in the music videos. I kept questioning if this was right, how was this modeling? I couldn't explain why, but I just knew something wasn't right. I was so uncomfortable, and the things he was saying as he was coaching me, and how he was looking at me, further confirmed what my gut was telling me. After the video, he told me that he was my manager and that nobody could know, especially not my mom. He said my mom would interfere and become a "stage mom" and make it difficult for me to win the contest and that nobody would want to work with me. He told me that if she found out, I would never be like the women in the catalogs. He sent the video off; well, at least he said he did. I didn't like how that experience felt, but I was going to be a model! I even told my friends; I was so excited! Sometime later, he came to me and said that I made it into the second round. To the mall we went again; this time though for bra and panties. Why? My "daddy" isn't supposed to take me to get bras and panties. None of my friend's dads took them, their moms did. The bra and panty set he picked out looked like something for my mom. Yes, I had enough to fill it in, but I was only eleven years old. He insisted that thirteen-year old girls in Europe wore this, and that they model like the ones in the catalog. He even commented to me that thirteen-year old girls could star in porn in Europe. I don't know what was more inappropriate, the fact that he made that comment to me or that fact that I knew what porn was. We made another video and this time I cried. I knew this wasn't right. He had to really sell me on it that day. We had to do so many takes because I kept looking scared. He kept yelling at me because I wasn't being sexy enough. I just wanted my mommy. Something wasn't right and I wasn't completely sure what. He was getting so angry with me; I just knew he was going to beat me. Instead, he grabbed me by the back of my neck and squeezed so tight that it seemed to paralyze me, or maybe it was just the fear in me. He then got in my ear and told me how ungrateful I was and how much he had to do to get me this opportunity. He threatened me and told me he would send me away to boarding school. After what seemed like an eternity and about a hundred takes. I did what he demanded. We weren't done though. He made me get on the bed and lie on my side across it, facing the camera and introduce my "manager." He then got on the bed behind me, still in only the white lace bra and panties he made me wear. He wrapped his arm around me and scooted in real close in a spooning manner. There was no space between us at all. He was pressed completely against the back of me, when he leaned in and kissed me on my jaw. I have literally blocked the rest of that moment from memory. I've even considered hypnosis to bring it back up, but I'm afraid of the impact it will have on me. That day changed me. I was no longer excited about modeling. I wanted out of it.

I contemplated suicide again; I contemplated telling my mom, but she was never on my side. I don't know if she feared him more, or just loved him more; all I know is that he and "his son", as he referred to him, mattered so much more to her than I did. Then one day my mom and that man called me into their room. He was standing on one side of the bed and she on the other. I could tell she had been crying and he looked infuriated. He was playing with these metal Chinese stress balls, like Lauwrence Fishburn had in the movie "Boyz n the Hood." He used those often to intimidate us. We knew when he had those in his hands that we better steer clear of him. He found out about mine and my mom's secret trip to meet my real dad. He made us feel so guilty about that and made us feel like we betrayed him. He told me that if I wanted a relationship with my real dad then I had to get out of his house. He was not about to "share" us. I was so confused; any other time he acted as if he didn't want me there. He would constantly tell me that I am her daughter and that he only has a son; unless we were around people, then I could never let anybody know he wasn't my real father. He and my mom had a huge fight that seemed to last for days. If he didn't hate me before, he definitely did now.

One day I was walking to the kitchen to get something to drink and he was at his desk on the phone. He stopped me and said, "turn around for a second, let me see your back." I knew not to deny him in front of anybody, so I just did what he said with no question. He then said to the person on the phone, "Oh yeah, baby got back!" He told me it was the modeling agency and that they wanted to fly me and him to Europe and again he emphasized that I could not tell my mom. He had me take the video up the street to the mailbox. The whole way there I wanted to trash it, but I feared him, so I didn't. I felt so violated. I knew what he meant and I knew he shouldn't be referring to me in that way. Yet I had no defense. That was also the time he began becoming angry when I would be around boys. He would react more like a jealous boyfriend than a "father." That's when it clicked: somehow, I knew that if I got the boys' interest, that he wouldn't like it. I don't know how, but I knew it would change how he saw me. I went after boys, full speed ahead. I turned on that "sexy" that he had taught me. I was always in some boys' face. I also discovered his porn collection. I wanted to know how to get and keep a boy's interest. I began watching them as a tutorial. If I was going to do this, I had to do it right. It wasn't long before I became addicted to pornography. At such a young age, I was already addicted to pornography. I would sneak and watch every time I was home alone. It started to control me completely. It was all I ever wanted to do. Then I began feeling like him: a creep and a pervert. Why was I watching this stuff? Why couldn't I stop watching this stuff?

He came to me to do another video and said that I made it into the finals. This time I had to be completely naked. He said this was the only way to take my measurements. Now, my second mom Hazel sewed, and I never saw her measure anybody on video or naked. I was helpless and by this point humiliated. My 'daddy' was about to see me naked. I felt so gross and after watching pornography, it became apparent to me how he was viewing me. I already felt a lot was wrong with this entire situation, but now knowing how adults interacted sexually, I knew he was not supposed to be interacting with me this way. He knew it too, yet he didn't cease to prey on me and violate me in such a way. This was so wrong! Why couldn't I stop him? Where was my mom? Why is he talking to me like that? I'm not "baby" or "gorgeous", I am your daughter. Somebody make it stop!

Not long after that I told him I didn't want to model anymore. I told him I didn't want to leave my mom and brother. He was so mad and shouted so many terrible things at me. He called me so many terrible names. I cried, I just cried!

Some time had passed, and he came to me and told me, I won that contest. I had absolutely no interest at this point. I saw right through him, he was just trying to get me to continue doing the videos. Something was in it for him, something he didn't want to lose. Something he didn't mind gaining at my expense. I knew it wasn't right at all. By that time, I had figured whatever he was doing with those videos, no child should've been a part of. He knew it and he knew that I knew it too.

## 11: BOY CRAZY

Chaos found its way back into the home, and I began Middle School. I was a completely different person than I was at the beginning of the summer. Daddy began calling me names like, slut and whore. I was beginning to see that, just maybe, his disdain was towards all females; not just me and mommy. I became familiar with the term chauvinist, and the fact that daddy was the true definition of such. Thirteen, finally a teenager! My mom and daddy let me have a party. I had a huge party! I got my hair done, and my first set of acrylics. I first spent the entire day getting pampered with my aunt and grandma; and then came home for my party - fashionably late, of course. My hair in a side ponytail with a swoop bang, my nails done, and the outfit that my Aunt Tonya purchased for me. I felt like one of the Fly Girls that danced on the show In Living Color. I couldn't wait for all of my friends to see me. This was about to be the best night of my life!

My mom greeted me as I walked up the driveway. She hugged me so tight, and told me she had something to tell me before I went inside. "Nikki, Richard, your dad, is back in jail." My heart sank; he would never rescue me now. Is this why I hadn't heard from him? She told me that she didn't know all the details, but that she was told he had been molesting my step-sister. Why was she telling me this now? Great! Another monster in my life; another pervert! I shrugged it off even though I wanted to cry. The party must go on. I was used to this kind of disappointment by now. I knew how to press through. So I did exactly that and I had the time of my life that night. We danced until we sweat our hair out and our clothes were drenched. Daddy was the DJ; he was good with music. We even had our garage turned into a recording studio. He spun all the hottest songs that were out, and he didn't play the edited versions. My friends kept talking about how cool my parents were. I felt accepted, and I felt so good, so normal. In that moment my parents were so cool to me too. Everyone at school talked about that party for literally years to come.

I also had sex for the first time that year. I could barely comb my own hair, but I was having sex. Doing some of the things I learned from watching his videos. I had been so accustomed to relating to males in a sexual way against my will that now the ability to choose gave me a sense of power. It also made me feel so grown up, but being grown up is what I had been forced to experience for quite some time by that point. I had a boyfriend three houses up and he was incredibly mean to me; like how daddy was to my mom. So it made me feel like I was in a real relationship, like we were a real couple. He would yell at me, cuss at me, push me, and order me around. This was exactly how it was supposed to be… right? I now had a real boyfriend. Though it had already been stolen in so many ways, he would be the one that I'd decided to give my virtue to. In my home, nobody talked to me about waiting or preserving my body. Everything that I had been forced to experience up to this point had taught me the exact opposite. My boyfriend was jealous too. Seeing me around boys made him so angry. My two friends and I had been hanging out with some other boys in the neighborhood. We all stopped by my boyfriend's house to see if he could come outside, but he wasn't home. We all went down to my friend's Jessilyn's house to play her Super Nintendo. My boyfriend found out where we were and stood outside of her front window screaming

"Nikki!" I went to the door and immediately he was in my face, screaming that I didn't have his permission to hang out with those boys. Then he turned to walk away; he was so upset. He turned back to me and slapped me so hard across my face. I was stunned. I had no time to defend myself. Was I supposed to defend myself? He cared for me, right? This was a sign of love... wasn't it? I found love! Didn't I?

One day, daddy asked me to ride with him to the mall; we didn't shop though. We went straight to the food court and sat down at a table. He wanted to talk to me. He was being strangely nice to me and asking me about my friends at school. He then asked me about the boy that lived three houses up. My heart started racing. He knew I had a boyfriend! What was he going to do to me here though? I didn't admit to anything; I felt as though I was being ambushed. He then took a large purple box of Trojan condoms out and sets them smack in the middle of the table. He said that he had found some of my poems, letters from my friends, and hate mail about him, which revealed my sexual activity. I was humiliated; everyone could see this box on the table. What was he doing? He didn't get upset though, and we had a pretty normal talk about practicing safe sex. He even assured me he wouldn't tell my mom. This was so strange. Were we having a real father-daughter moment, in the food court over a huge box of condoms? We laughed and he listened to me talk about boys and school. I enjoyed it, yet it was foreign to me. After a while, I noticed this look on his face: it was a look that made me feel like I had just gotten bamboozled. I felt setup and I shut up. Checkmate, Shawnetta. Whatever it was that was brewing would rear its ugly head sooner or later. I owed him now because he had something on me that my mom didn't know about. He would, definitely, want the favor returned - some way or another.

Mid-way through the first semester my favorite cousin Toni came to live with me. No one, not even family, had any clue how horrible my home life was. So when things got tough for Toni in Utah, the family truly felt she would be better off living in Cali with us. After all, she had spent time with us a couple of summers before and all was well. That was a huge mistake, although, now I wasn't in this fight alone. I couldn't wait to get her acquainted with all my friends; and then she made some of her own. My circle grew with her around and my idea of fun changed. We began hanging out on the Eastside of town drinking, smoking weed, stealing, having sex, and fighting. Being at parties with Tanguray gin on our breath, marijuana filling up our lungs, fights breaking out, bullets flying past us, and running from the Sheriff's department as they came to grab all of us up out of the streets was the new definition of good times. If our night didn't end with us hiding behind a building or in a field trying to catch our breath after running away from bullets or the cops, then we weren't satisfied.

During this time, I became more bold and promiscuous. Daddy was becoming angrier because I wasn't living in fear anymore and he didn't like it. He zoned in on Toni and our relationship. He despised the fact that I had her and drew strength from her. With her around, I walked differently and talked differently. He couldn't intimidate me or control me as he had before she came. He put us on a buddy system so that whenever someone got in trouble for any reason, then we would both get beat. That system didn't work to his advantage, but instead to ours. It strengthened our alliance even more and weakened his hold on us. One night he was upset about the way she spoke to my younger brother after he told on us for sneaking our friends into the house. My brother was always trying to get us in trouble. He got rewarded for it, and I began to resent him for it. No matter what I tried to bribe him with, his alliance with his father was too strong to break. Daddy stood us in the middle of my brother's room forcing us to apologize to him. He began yelling at her and calling her all kinds of names. He was all in her face and spit was flying onto both of us as I stood next to her. Before I could catch myself, I spoke up and said, "she's not your child, you can't talk to her like that." I could feel the rage rising up in him almost instantly. He hated that I stood up to him, and at the defense of someone else. Then she chimed in in agreement. He could no longer contain his composure and he yelled out in a booming voice, "I will talk to either of you little bitches how in the fuck ever I want to in my goddamn house!" Then he slapped her so hard that it knocked her in between my brother's bunk bed and dresser. I screamed, "Don't hit her!" and he started throwing punches at me. The first one knocked me down and once I was down, he kept wailing on my head and face and kicking me in my ribs. I just wasn't taking it this time. I don't know what came over me, but I fought back. My cousin jumped on his back screaming and then we all three spilled out into the hallway; hair flying, blood dripping, screaming, crying, and gasping for air because we had gotten winded from the impact of the body shots he was slamming into our guts. I felt like I was fighting someone at school. My mom tried to break up the fighting, which then caused her to be the target. She never called the police though. It was just another day in the household. I was so furious with my mom about that. It was one thing to let him beat me, but to let him beat her like that; allowing that three-hundred-pound man to fight us like grown men, and we each weighed about ninety pounds, at best. Toni's family entrusted her into their care, and this was the kind of "care" she receieved. The beatings only increased and intensified from that day. He was no longer slapping, but now punching, kicking, and pulling hair. No longer was I the target, now we both were. He was relentless; I was rebellious, and mommy was helpless. I couldn't write because he would find it. He considered my writing to be hate mail, as he called it, and I would get beat every time he found it. I couldn't go to therapy because they wouldn't take me that far. I couldn't have sex all day and every day because I no longer had the freedom to be around boys whenever I wanted. What outlet would I have to cope? I loved dancing since before I could remember, and my cousin also expressed an interest in it. So when mommy and daddy told us to pick an activity we chose that, but they refused to drive us to the dance school we wanted to attend. Mommy and daddy said we could choose what we wanted, but daddy had other plans. He made it clear that we would have to do whatever my younger brother wanted to do. My cousin and I were forced into Tae Kwon Do, kind of as a punishment of some sort. Daddy wanted us to hate it and to be miserable doing it. My cousin and I cried the first day of class. Standing there in our white uniforms, wanting to run out the door and never come back. It was awful; well at first it was. Once I realized I was going to get to fight without getting in trouble, I was completely sold. My cousin also took to it, but not with the same passion as me. It proved to be so therapeutic for me. I didn't need the boys and I didn't need the booze. A healthy way to release my anger and frustration is what I needed. I ended up excelling at it: I had found my outlet! I competed, won a ton of trophies, and eventually got my blackbelt. Daddy's plan was foiled: this wasn't punishment for me at all. He'd soon fix me though. It was like he was always making a point to express how proud he was of his son and how Nikki could do better. What was better than first place? No matter how many first place trophies I came home from competition with, I still wasn't celebrated the same way. He then started accusing us of stealing money from him. It was so calculated, as if he needed a reason to beat us up. Too much time had gone by and he needed his fix. He came in our room accusing us of stealing money. When we denied it, he made us start looking for two hundred dollars. He left the house and said if we didn't put it back by the time he came back home he was going to beat us. We didn't find it, and we tore that house up - all twelve hundred square feet. We even looked in the attic. He came home and we had no money for him. "I know you little bitches stole my shit", he yelled. He grabbed me by my hair first and then by her hair. He flung us around and started throwing punches at us. He beat us down and then went to bed. The next day when he got home from work, he said to us "I found my money; I had it in my car." Never an apology; just went about business as usual. Something inside of me told me that he knew we didn't have that money. Why did he hate us so much? Why was he happiest when he was hurting us? After that, I went right back into my reckless spiral, seeking out acceptance - male acceptance. If it wasn't boys, it was booze. Those seemed to be the only two things to soothe me.

Summer came and my cousin Toni was gone; he sent her away to hurt me. He beat her, broke her, then disposed of her. Why couldn't I have gone with her? On our way home from visiting friends in Simi Valley, mom and daddy got into an argument in the car. They were arguing about something he said to me, and out of nowhere he slammed my mom's head into the passenger window. They tussled a little bit before he pulled over and mom got out of the car and started walking. He called for her to get back in and she kept walking. He sped off; he was leaving her. "Don't leave my mom out here," I said; "you can't leave her. I want my mom!" I started crying. He started mocking me and making fun of my concern and tears; "fuck your mom and fuck you," he said and then chuckled. There was no way I was going anywhere with him without my mom. I unbuckled my seatbelt and lunged towards the driver seat and screamed in his ear, "Go get my mom!" He elbowed me in my face, slammed on the breaks, turned around and started punching me in the backseat. "You bastard," he yelled; "nobody gives a shit about you or her." With my hands up, trying to protect my face, I slumped down in my seat and just cried. While waiting out the flurry of punches and slaps, my brother started crying which probably saved my life. He stopped hitting me and just sat in the driver's seat catching his breath. He then went back and got her. I didn't say a word the whole ride home. I just cried, and so did she.

One summer afternoon, I was hanging out with one of my friends from school. She lived down the street from me, near the park. Her friend was visiting from the East Coast and they were home alone. We decided to sample some things from her dad's liquor cabinet. The sampling turned into complete debauchery. We were completely wasted; stumbling, laughing, running around like crazy and vomiting; completely out of control. On that day something awakened inside of me. Something that had been there for quite some time and I just never realized it. In my mind, I went back to that day playing house with blue-eyes; I then went to that day that daddy told me I was gay. Maybe he was right because the desire that came over me for my friend confirmed what he accused me of that day. I was so intoxicated, more than I had ever been before. I had no clue what I was doing, or even if I really wanted to be doing it. I was no longer in control of my actions or thoughts. Sometime later, her younger sister came home and found us passed out, naked and covered in vomit. I remember her crying and thinking we were dead. She bathed each of us and cleaned us up before their dad came home. Sick with what I was sure was alcohol poisoning, I spent the next few days piecing together what occurred. Finally, all the fuzzy pieces flooded my memory in clear HD quality and the tears of shame soaked my face. It was clear as day playing in my mind: that day I had an experience with her; an experience that was too much and at the same time just enough; enough to fuel my curiosity; further confusing me, and for years to come tormenting me with shame. I didn't know what it was at the time, but every time I had been violated those spirits had been planted in me: that perverse spirit, that violent spirit, and that abusive spirit. I sexed, partied, and fought. I was so promiscuous and angry. The angrier I became, the more promiscuous I became. Then the more promiscuous I became, the angrier I became. I believed everything daddy told me. I believed that I was a whore, that I was a bitch, and that all I had to offer anybody was my body. At the tender age of thirteen, I believed it and I became it; all of it, and I hated it. I hated myself.

## 12: UNPOPULAR POPULARITY

I'm in High School! What a different world from Junior High. I was literally fascinated with everyone my eyes came across. I wanted to be a little bit of everyone – everyone, but me. I was so depressed; my self-esteem was so low. My two best friends distanced themselves from me, embarrassed by my reputation. Despite my reputation, I was pretty, popular, and I did make other friends; friends that also evolved into family. Still, those two friends pulling away from me hurt, and would put a strain on our friendship for years to come. Have you ever felt loved and hated with the same exact intensity? That is what high school felt like for me. I struggled with being liked and being hated; wanting to be loved and feeling like nobody cared; needing to be free and to be me, but at the same time hating who I was.

I had several boyfriends in high school. I really liked them all, but was never sure if they liked me or were using me. Mostly though, I just needed to feel wanted, and to have someone to feed my addiction, so if they were using me, it didn't bother me for that long. Having at least one other person always made me feel a little less guilty about my sexual activity. Which was one of the reasons I tried to hold onto each of my relationships with those boys. In addition to physical needs, I needed them to like me, to accept me, to desire me, to be there for me, protect me, and to prove to myself that I was worthy and beautiful enough to have any of them claim me as their girl. My insecurities and need to have a boy on my arm seemed to make me the center of the rumor mill. I was never the only promiscuous girl, nor was I the most out there, yet the rumors about me seemed so much more hurtful and vile than what was heard about many of my peers. Maybe it seemed so much worse in my mind because, for me, I was secretly battling so much already. I was always defending myself at school and at home, both physically and verbally. I was defending myself against daddy, against my peers, and myself. I was tired: tired of fighting, tired of drinking, tired of crying, tired of hiding and tired of living. It was time to go. No note, no goodbyes. We were on break from school and everyone was gone. I was home alone. Lynae and Jessilyn had boyfriends and new best friends, who they were spending more time with. I took some pills and chased them with some alcohol from a couple of nights prior that I was able to purchase at a local gas station that didn't card us. I felt light; the heaviness on my heart was disappearing. I hadn't felt this free in as long as I could remember. Everything went black. I woke up hung-over and feeling like even more of a failure. I couldn't even kill myself right! I cried and I wrote, and then cried some more. I was so pathetic; no wonder everyone hated me.

Just before my sixteenth birthday, on a bus ride home from summer school, I met a boy sitting in the back whom I'd never seen before. Was he new here? We made eye contact, but he didn't say a word to me the entire ride. "5th street west", called out the driver. This was my stop. As I got up to prepare to exit, the boy sitting in the back said to me, "hey white v-neck, can I get your number?" I quickly jotted it down and got off the bus. As I walked up the hill, to my house, I wondered if he would call me. He was really cute and he had hypnotizing eyes, I thought. Something else about him struck me though, and he had only said a few words. He didn't come at me like all the other guys I'd met. He even had a maturity to him - was he older than me? I had so many questions; why didn't he start talking to me as soon as I got on the bus? I felt a connection that I had never experienced before was there with Mr. Bus Stop, and I couldn't wait to find out more about it. His name was JD, and about a month after meeting him, and only seeing him one more time; he had to go away. Not forever though.

For the remainder of high school, I continued to fight at home and at school. I continued to feed my addictions. I learned how to put on a mask. I learned how to smile through my pain. I enjoyed the friends I did have, and tried my best to ignore the rest. One person that stood out was probably the only girl shorter than me. Asha and I met in chorus and were inseparable from day one. Asha, her brother, and his best friend. They never judged me and never switched up on me. No matter what was being spread around about me, I truly felt like they loved me and accepted me. We became family, all of us. I had psychology class with Asha's brother and his best friend. Some of my best high school memories were created with them in that class. I didn't know it at the time, Asha and her brother were coping with some heavy things at home as well; so it was as if he knew what I was going through without me saying a word. Like my energy was a familiar energy to him. I'd sit next to him in class and he'd jokingly acknowledge my bruises as if they were from another fight at school. He knew the truth though, and many years later before he died, he let me know that he did.

Senior year was almost through. I had almost made it through high school. JD, Mr. Bus Stop, was back, but just as a friend at first; but it was definitely blossoming into something more. He lived far, so we didn't see each other much; we just wrote letters and talked on the phone. I was getting at least two letters a week from him. It was as if I could talk to him about anything... well, almost anything. JD motivated and encouraged me, unlike anyone else. It was a connection that was so pure and so sound, and not based on sex because we had not been physical with each other at this point. The most genuine connection I had ever had with any guy before.

College acceptance letters were in and I didn't get accepted into UCLA, which was devastating, but my high school counselor let me know that CSUN was going to be my new home. I had gotten into college! I was heading down to take my entrance exam and I was so excited. I could picture the dorms in my head, and I could see myself in my lectures taking notes. I was ready for this. I was finally getting out of that city and that house. Life was going to be great. My bubble was quickly busted when daddy started ridiculing me, belittling me and calling me all sorts of names. He had just helped me get my prom dress and was acting like a normal father, which he did periodically, and it always left me emotionally and mentally confused. Now he was on a war path, again. I don't even remember what he was upset about, but I'll never forget how he made me feel that day. It was so calculated, almost like he was trying to get into my head before this big test. He wanted me to go in there with a defeated mindset. It worked; I felt like a failure before I even sat down. I couldn't even take my exam. I filled out almost the entire scantron without even reading more than two or three of the actual questions. He was right: I felt worthless. I wasn't going to college, especially to that college. I made up my mind what I was going to do. I was so smart, got good grades, and I was talented at dance and track, but in that moment, I decided that I wanted to be a stripper or a porn star. I didn't care how short life was, even in spite of the multiple friends that had passed away in high school. I wanted fast money and I wanted to make it doing what I felt I was good at, what I felt was the only thing I was worth, what daddy told me I was. I was really going to be popular now. Lack of acceptance would no longer be a struggle for me.

## 13: HIM OR ME

After graduation, I attended the local Junior College where I just partied and continued to be promiscuous and self-destructive. One night, shortly after my 18th birthday, a guy I was dating came by the house to talk to me. While I was talking to my guy, he noticed daddy periodically peering through the blinds at us. He was a little intimidated, but I assured him it was nothing. We continued to talk and hugged and kissed. We were just soaking in the warm night breeze. The smell of freshly cut grass was in the air and the slight mist of water from the sprinklers was dancing around us. Then daddy came out of the house yelling, "Nikole, get in the house it's late!" It was only nine pm, so I brushed him off and kept talking. I'm eighteen now he can't do anything to me. He storms across the lawn to where I was and yanks my arm and said, "Get in the motherfucking house now!" I snatch my arm away. Why was he out here acting like a jealous boyfriend? It was the strangest thing. He was completely fine before my friend came over, at least it seemed that way. He yanked me by my hair and took me down onto the grass and started dragging me by my hair into the house. I was kicking and screaming, and yelled for my friend to leave. I was screaming, "let me go, let me fucking go!" He didn't, he just kept dragging me, all the way into the house. He slammed the door and started pummeling me with his fist on my head. After a while I couldn't feel my head anymore; I couldn't feel my soul anymore. It was like I left my body. He punched, kicked, and swung, until he ran out of breath, but he didn't let go of me. Blood was running down my face all-of-a-sudden and I could feel pain everywhere. I screamed. With all of myself that I could pull together, I hollered. My mom pulled him off me and she was, yelling at me, "Nikki what did you do? Damn it, Shawnetta, why? What did you do?" It was as if this just had to be my fault. That's how we were conditioned by him though, never to blame him, but always us. They walked into the hallway, she was crying and he was trying to catch his breath. They were arguing. I limped into the kitchen and grabbed the sharpest chef knife out of the knife block. "What the fuck do you think you're doing?" he taunted me and then let out this sinister laugh, challenging me it seemed. I screamed, "That's the last time you put your hands on me, I'm going to kill you!" and ran towards him knife in hand. He screeched so loud, that he sounded like a woman; I'd never heard his voice reach that octave before. I scared him; he was so afraid, and that was so empowering to me. I was going to kill him, and it felt good. All the years of abuse, violation, intimidation, hurt, torture, was all about to end right there, right then. We wrestled over the knife, and then my mom jumped into help him. Was she crazy?! I'm doing this for us, so he can't hurt us anymore; I thought to myself. They got the knife away from me, and I lost it. All the years of hurt came pouring out of me, and I couldn't stop it. I went into the cabinet and got the bottle of Aspirin and downed it right there with them looking at me. They both came rushing towards me: "Shawnetta no!" If he wasn't going to die, I was! They tackled me to the ground as I began chewing the pills since I couldn't swallow them fast enough. The bitter taste of the pills made me gag, but I was determined, so I kept chewing. I chewed like my life depended on it, or more like my death depended on it. He held me down while my mom fished everything out of my mouth. She was so determined that she hardly flinched when I began biting her fingers. She just hit me until I let go and kept fishing out the pills. They left me on the floor in a ball, crying hysterically, and went and called the police. My mom was given a choice by the officers that night: him or me. All she had to do was tell them the truth. Tell them about the hell we endured. Send him to jail; this time let him stay there. She didn't choose though. She copped out and just walked away. She left me standing there with daddy and the police. The was the most abandoned I had ever felt in my life. That moment gave life to the abandonment issues that had been lying dormant inside of me. Daddy decided my fate that night, and it wasn't in my favor. He attacks me, she calls the police, and I'm the one that had to go.

I was cast out and cut off. I couldn't even talk to my little brother. Daddy wouldn't let me. I stayed around the corner with my Lynae's family and began looking for stripping jobs. I was on a mission, and now I needed the money. I grabbed a paper and started circling random jobs. I think I started to second guess my decision. I started to worry about what people would say if they found out. I called JD. He helped me to get over that worry; he seemed to be down for me no matter what. If only he lived closer, we could be together. He was perfect for me, he understood me, and never judged me. I loved our talks; he had a way of calming my fears and making everything make sense. With confidence, I continued my search. In big bold red letters there it was in the classified ads; just what I was looking for. I called the number, met with the owner the next day, and within a week was doing house calls. It was perfect; nobody would run into me in a club. Nobody would see me out and about. They would only know if I told them. I was an escort; not exactly a stripper but close enough at the time. I would get a page from the company when a request came in. I had a driver/bodyguard that would pick me up from home and take me on all my calls and stayed outside waiting for me. My first call I was a nervous wreck; a complete fumbling fool. "How hard could this be, Shawnetta?" I asked myself. Just dance around for an hour, make a little conversation, get paid, and go home. I quickly got the hang of it though; maybe a little too much, because now I was doing much more than conversation and stripteases. I had clients in different cities and from all walks of life: old men, young men, single men, married men, couples, corporate employees, business owners, college professors and college athletes. I did parties or one on one. Nobody could tell me nothing. I had regular clients, some of them with standing appointments. The money was great, so great, that when the opportunity to make more came, I jumped at it. I learned how to maximize my money and make the most of my time. I was raking in the dough and only going out a few days a week. This was the life... or was it? I still felt so empty, and started to feel dirty. I'd look in the mirror and the person looking back at me sickened me. I had money to spend now and hole in my heart and a hole in my pocket. A new addiction was forming, and I missed my mommy and my brother. Daddy won, she let him. We couldn't beat him if we tried. There was absolutely nothing I could do to take away this hurt. Well, actually there was one thing: hello, retail therapy.

## 14: BACK WHERE I STARTED

Mid-November was here; I couldn't believe how fast the last couple of months flew by. My mom came by to see me one day, and I knew it wasn't good. We hadn't even spoken since I left the house - well, since I was put out. My great grandmother was gone. My Sammy was not with us anymore. She had battled many years with her health and her body couldn't take it anymore. My heart broke into a million pieces as I collapsed onto the couch. I sat there reflecting on all the Christmases, Family reunions, and many other visits to her home in Salt Lake City. The precious time and memories I had with her, were all I had left of her. I sat there and just cried. Who knew I had any tears left? She also told me that my grandpa and grandma Datha wanted me to come live with them in order to get myself together, and that my aunt Tonya had a job opportunity for me. With Lynae not speaking to me anymore, and me failing out of school, the only things holding me here was JD and escorting - which was getting to me in the worst way. JD lived so far, and we never saw each other. We promised to stay in touch, and I said my goodbyes. I was going back home, back to the Bay. My first stop was Salt Lake City, Utah. That funeral was so hard. To have a wake, Thanksgiving, and then the funeral in a three-day period was so hard on our entire family. A ray of light, shined on me through the dark clouds though when JD told me that he loved me, while we were talking on the phone. I couldn't believe my ears. No guy I'd ever dated said those three words, and we weren't even dating. He had never been with me physically, and I wasn't his girl, yet he was saying those magical words to me. I needed those words, and they awakened something in me. In that moment, he tapped into and grabbed a hold of my very soul. A grasp he'd have for many years to come. Right then though, he became my man and he loved me.

Oakland, California; December 1998. I pulled up onto 50th Ave to one of my favorite places in the world: my grandpa John and grandma Datha's house; my new home. It was a little different, she wasn't in the kitchen cooking for the week. The house didn't smell of culinary greatness. I was used to walking in and seeing her in the kitchen preparing meals for the week. I was used to fresh baked cakes and pies across the countertop. She loved to cook, and was amazing at it. Grandma Datha wasn't in the kitchen cooking though, and she wasn't her lively self. She wasn't even able to walk to the front of the house to greet me. She wasn't strong enough, because her cancer was back, and this time it was really, aggressive. She still greeted me with that beautiful smile and girlish giggle. Her presence was so warm - as always; his not so much, he was stern and tough. He was very critical, and at times even mean, yet there was nothing he wouldn't do for me. Here I was in another new city, another fresh start. The difference this time is now I have a chip on my shoulder. My family thought I wasn't ready for this city, but this city wasn't ready for me; so I thought. I had an agenda. The first week I was there I got hired at a dental office and a department store - thanks to my aunt Tonya. I also enrolled in school for the spring semester. I was doing pretty well at first. I was in my Biology class when this tall girl came in and said, "is this Biology 101?" I told her she was in the right place and we just began talking. Since I had just moved back and was still adjusting, she wanted me to come hang out after class. From that moment on we were inseparable. Tatiana and I were all over the place, doing everything. I got back into stripping and was still working at a dental office. My seasonal position at the department store was up, so I got a second job at the beauty supply Tatiana worked at. We hustled! We were into everything; some of it illegal and some not. I was still in a long distance relationship with JD and made a trip to Los Angeles to see him for Valentine's weekend. I went straight to USC to see one of my best friends, Leigh, that was in school there. Leigh and I had known each other since freshman year of high school-but became very close our senior year. My boyfriend stood me up the first night. I was devastated. I had been looking forward to this weekend for months and now he wasn't answering his phone or responding to my pages. What happened to love? Did he not love me anymore?

That night Leigh and I decided to have an impromptu dorm party. Booze was always good for cheering me up. We loaded up on liquor and before we knew it, her room was full of drunken young men and women. Music was blasting and people were staggering and running from one dorm room to the next. Everyone was having so much fun. It was exactly what I needed to distract me from my hurt feelings. Two men mentioned they had some weed in their room. They seemed nice and weren't showing any attraction or interest in me, so I felt it was safe to go with them. Everything was fine. These guys were harmless college students-weren't they? We smoked and talked about school, sports and our relationships. They sat on one side of the room and I sat on the other. They never gave me any reason to feel unsafe or uncomfortable. They didn't flirt or make any passes at me. Then I passed out. I woke up in a pitch black room. The room was spinning, and my vision was blurry. I saw a shadow over me and as my eyes adjusted to the darkness, I noticed it was one of the young men. Something wasn't right, and then my body started to wake up. I was feeling everything; I felt pain. He was panting; I began crying and saying "no." I begged for him to get off of me. I had a boyfriend and I didn't consent to this. I couldn't believe what was happening. I was trying to fight him off, but my arms were so weak. I was so drunk and high. I was defenseless. I begged and begged, he covered my mouth and whispered, "Shut the hell up man, I'm almost done." My cries were muffled by his hand and as he tightened his grip over my mouth. Then I passed out again. I woke up the next morning with a massive headache. I turned and saw a stranger lying next to me, naked. I felt my body for my clothes. Everything from the waist down was gone and the memory of what happened flooded my mind. I screamed and jumped up. I kicked him to wake him up. "You raped me!" He tried to explain, but there was no explanation; I had said no. I was defenseless and begging him to stop. He was a monster; he had to be to take it from me the way he did. How could I let him do that to me? I hurried and put my clothes back on, but I wanted to burn them; I wanted to burn my whole body. I felt disgusting and awful. How could I be so stupid? I should've fought harder, screamed louder, or bit his hand or something. I was ashamed and embarrassed. Everything daddy ever told me played in my head. I began blaming myself. Maybe I deserved it. Nobody would believe a girl like me. I had a reputation of being promiscuous; they would say I asked for it. I decided not to tell anyone the truth. Instead, I returned to my Leigh's room and when she asked where I had been all night, I simply said, "I got lost." We made a joke of that, and it stuck for many years, but what happened to me was no laughing matter.

That rape and JD standing me up, killed a part of me. I felt raped by two men; my attacker, for the obvious reasons, and my man for not being there when I needed him. Had he been there, it would've never happened. How could I disassociate him from such a horrible event? I couldn't, and for many years to come I wouldn't.

When I returned to Oakland I was numb. JD and I eventually broke up. I began dating drug dealers, male strippers, rappers, business owners and gangsters. I even dated a guy that I later found out ran with the crew that tried to kill my uncle, but it didn't stop me from dating him. I needed him; I needed them all. It was like each man got me further and further away from the man that raped me and the one that broke my heart. I was on my kick again, chasing that high. Money, alcohol, and men were my drug of choice. I stayed with a fully stocked supply.

One of those men I dated was a Muslim man I met at a club one night. Muhair wasn't as tall as I preferred, but his confidence made him appear to be the tallest man in the room. He was so handsome - almost beautiful. I was so intrigued and so attracted. I didn't ask what he did for a living; I was only concerned if he had enough money to keep up with me. My thing back then was if you couldn't do more for me than I could do for myself, we had no business talking. I never asked anybody specifics though; if I found out it was because the information was offered to me. One night, Muhair wanted to go into the city of San Francisco and said he had to take care of some business and wanted me to go with him. The first stop we made was at a barber shop; he had me come in and proudly introduced me to everyone as his girl. I was on cloud nine; he had so much power and respect. In my mind he could have any woman and he chose me. He went into the back with a couple of people and had a young white girl sit with me. She didn't talk much, even though I tried to engage her; she seemed a bit afraid. It was strange, but I didn't read much into it. Besides, she was high, and that I was certain of. He came out and we left; the young white girl came with us. He made a few phone calls as we drove to another stop and picked up another girl. Still not thinking much of it, I just relaxed into the front seat and went along for the ride. The two girls began talking about an incident with some man and another girl. I made small talk with him as I pretended to not be paying attention to them. What I heard made it clear what this situation was: they were hoes. The working kind and my man was their pimp. I began thinking, "what is this?" I know he's not about to try to pull me into this. I worked for Shawnetta only. When I wanted, how I wanted, and I wasn't about to give any money I earned to some pimp. He dropped off the second girl we had picked up at another complex. As we were riding, he began telling the first girl that he was upset with her speaking about business in front of me. I don't remember exactly what all was said, but she got a little mouthy with him. Before I knew it, he pulled over quickly. I hardly blinked an eye before he had snatched her out of the car by her hair and onto the sidewalk. I jumped out to intervene and then noticed a gun in Muhair's hand. He shook his head at me real slow and I knew not to even utter a sound. He beat her up so bad on that sidewalk, and I could do was pray that he didn't kill her or me; and then left her there in the rain. He called someone to pick her up, and commented on how her mouth messed up his money, because now she can't go out with her face all beat up. Was he serious? She may need a doctor, and he was worried about her not being able to make him some money. This was a side of him that I hadn't seen before and I didn't like it. How quickly he went from being calm to being so violent and angry, reminded me of daddy, and it terrified me. I just wanted to get back across that bridge safely! He carried on as if nothing happened and I tried to act as natural as possible. Once he got me home, I never answered another one of his calls again. He called so much and left so many messages at first. Then the calls just stopped.

Tatiana and I got hired to do a birthday party for the brother of one of the strippers we knew. It was at a hotel in Jack London Square. When we got there, two other strippers were there, but she wanted them to go first. She told us that we were the big finale for her brother and his friends. They were all the way live in there. I took a couple of shots to loosen up, but she didn't drink. The two women went first, and then Alluzion and China Doll closed out. We shut it down. They were ballers, street cats, but balling out of control.

They were throwing twenties and hundreds at us. Then the sister mysteriously disappeared. She was cheering us on and throwing money one second, and then gone the next. I got a weird feeling, but I ignored it. Our time was almost up and we were getting way too much money to quit now. That's when one of the men put the music on pause and said, "Now we really finna have a party up in here." Before I knew it, three men were on her and I was surrounded by four or five with two of them pulling me onto the bed. They were touching us and taking things too far. We were both struggling and pleading for them to stop. A few of the men standing around were taking their clothes off. They were getting ready to rape us, and one whispered in my ear, "you see all these niggas in here, you bet not get loud, or we gonna silence the both of you hoes." That's when we heard banging on the door; a few of the men ran to it, while others held us down. It was the other two strippers. One of the girls left her bag. They let them in and let us up and we hurried and grabbed our clothes and money. They weren't the type to do something like that and let us get away to tell. I didn't want them to think I was going to snitch so I said, "Happy Birthday!

Thanks for having us." And said, "holla at us for the next one." Just like that we were out. There was an eerie silence between us as we walked to our car. It seemed as if not a single person was out that night. It was strange because that part of town is usually buzzing, but now it was dead silent. I felt death and I didn't have a doubt in my mind about it. We just escaped death, and it was so scary. See, it's a different feeling when you aren't in control of whether you live or die. Then I said, "I'm done; they would've killed us." She agreed. As we walked, we both cried silently. The tears fell, and we just walked. When we made it back to her car, we vowed never to speak of it with each other again.

A few days later Tatiana confessed to me that she was only seventeen and a senior in High School. I was furious; I was nineteen going on twenty. I was responsible for her and could've gotten into so much trouble had anything happened to her. All this time and all this dirt?! Things were spiraling out of control during this time, and I was spiraling right with them.

Right in the midst of all the craziness that was my life at this time, there came the news that one of my closest friends since seventh grade, passed away in a terrible car accident along with four other people. Two of them I also knew very well. My whole entire world just crumbled. When I got the call, I screamed so loud it echoed throughout the neighborhood. My whole body went limp, and my mom's voice seemed so far in the background. I wasn't even holding the phone anymore. I had just talked to him three days before when I went to Palmdale to visit. He invited me to go with them that day, but I knew I would already be back home and couldn't go. This could not be real. My grandma Datha was getting more and more sick, my friend was dead, I was destroying myself and I was so depressed. That funeral was the hardest thing I had ever had to face up to that point in my life. I was on edge. That death, although not the first, was one of the most difficult for me. I was having suicidal thoughts again. Then one night, while feeding my pet tarantula, some of the crickets got out. That scared my grandma Datha, and me because we couldn't stand crickets. My aunt confronted me about it and I just lost it. Something so minor, but I went completely off and downed almost an entire bottle of pills that I had in my room. "Nikki what are you so mad about, why are you always so unhappy?!" she asked me. "I don't know, and I don't care anymore!" I yelled back at her. My aunt forced me to go to the ER that night. She said if I was going to do that to myself, it wouldn't be on her watch or in my grandparents' home.

At the hospital, they made me drink charcoal and told me if I didn't, that they would pump my stomach. In my mind, I couldn't understand what all the fuss was about. Somebody wants to die let them, let me. At that time, it hadn't ever occurred to me how selfish I was being. I was so focused on who didn't love me, and I didn't give those who did a second thought. I was so focused on all that I didn't have, that I was completely blind to all that I did have. I just wanted the pain I felt to go away forever. I wanted to go home, so I could kill myself when nobody was around to stop me; so I began drinking the charcoal. Drinking that stuff was horrible and then it all started to come back up. I couldn't stop throwing up. The taste of cabbage, bacon, fried chicken, bile, and charcoal didn't make it any better. I wanted to die even more then. They cleaned me up, and just when I thought I was going home, in came an officer to take me to the Psych Hospital. "Where's my aunt?" I said. I just knew she would not let them take me. "Get my aunt in here; she isn't going to let you take me like this!" She had left though, and she did let them take me. The counselor doing my intake, kept asking me if I wanted to die and I kept telling her yes. After the fifth time, I got agitated and snapped at her, "yes, I want to die; I hate this place, I hate my life. The answer is yes!" She scooted her chair in closer to me and leaned in and said, "Look, once you go upstairs, you aren't leaving. I can tell you're special though, which is why I'm giving you the chance to get out of here. Anybody else would've went straight upstairs after the first yes." I didn't see what she saw or why she saw it, or if she really saw anything at all. I knew that she didn't want me there, and I didn't want to be there. Her voice and her words still resonate with me today.

I had some peace for a while; it didn't last long though. My aunts came into my room one day to let me know that Tatiana got caught messing with one of my aunt's men. All hell seemed to break loose in the family because they thought I knew. They shut me out and called me disloyal. I was so hurt; I didn't understand how her decisions brought blame and shame on me. I felt so cast out by my family; first my mom and brother, now my two aunts; my friends all hundreds of miles away. It seemed like I had no one left except Tatiana. So, I continued with the friendship. The craziness didn't stop there, she got into a fight with aunt Tonya, while picking up my paycheck for me because I had called out sick. I got fired and my aunts stopped speaking to me altogether. I became angry and isolated. My mentality was, why did I have to lose my job over the decisions of two other people and their lack of self-control. I wasn't even there. I wasn't acknowledging the fact that I had brought Tatiana into our lives, therefore I did hold some of the responsibility for what all went down. I really needed to make a choice and some changes, but I wasn't ready to.

The holidays were here, but Christmas cheer wasn't necessarily being spread. Exactly seven days before Christmas, my grandma Datha won her fight against cancer. Surrounded by family, in her home, she went on to glory. I stayed by her hospice bed for what seemed like an eternity. She was still warm as I held her hand and smoothed her hair. I thanked her for everything. I just talked to her and told her how much I loved her.

How much I appreciated her love for me, even though I wasn't biologically her grandchild. Then my Grandpa John came in asked for some time alone. I stood by the door for a moment and watched him. Partially concerned and partially intrigued because I'd never seen him so sad, he was broken. That was the first time I ever saw my grandpa John cry. Not long after that, I moved in with another relative, who also lived in Oakland.

One night, Tatiana insisted I get out, so we went to this sports bar in Emeryville. We got in pretty much everywhere we went. We either had a fake ID or one of us was messing with the bouncer and we would get let in. But we had ID's this particular night. She had just started dating this guy named Ro, he was a computer geek, a fine one at that, and worked in Silicon Valley. They introduced me to his best friend Tory - equally as fine and equally as paid. He worked in Silicon Valley too. A much needed change in pace for me from the street dudes and strippers I was hanging with. He was ten, almost eleven years, older than me, but we had a ball. I wanted for nothing. He catered to me so much. He was so good to me, at least at first.

I worked registry for a dental office, worked at the beauty supply and assisted my friend while she did hair. We had a sweet hustle going. I felt like I was making so much money; but I was spending it just as fast as I was making it. I was even getting custom clothes made by an up and coming local designer; plus my boyfriend was pulling in six figures. I couldn't be told anything. I did what I wanted, with whom I wanted, how I wanted, no matter how bad it was. I was just reckless, entitled, and set out to get whatever I wanted without giving much for it. I acted like the world owed me something for the hell I'd been through. This was my crutch and I used it often to get what I wanted. My mentality was: "What's mine is mine, and what's yours is mine."

On my way back from one of our weekly shopping sprees, my friend was driving so fast. Since I lost my friend in that car accident, I was very leery about people driving reckless. I kept asking her to slow down, and I was getting upset. I just wanted to get home safe, and she kept taunting me to smile. I was in no mood to smile, I was scared and just wanted her to slow down. She didn't slow down at all though. Instead she began driving more reckless, and before we knew it the car was in pieces on the 580 freeway. We wrecked. All I could see was white smoke; I couldn't hear or feel anything. "Am I dead?" I wondered. Then Korrupt and Nate Dogg could be heard in the background. I could then see the glass within an inch of my face. Everything hurt all at once. I could hear people saying, "Are they dead?" "Can you hear us in there?" "Call 911." I could then hear Tatiana whisper, "Shawn." I jumped out of the car so fast; I had to know if I was alive. My dress was torn; blood was running from several places. "Get her out! Help her out!" I screamed. Bystanders helped me to the side of the freeway and sat me down. I tried to get back up to see about my friend. One woman said, "sweetie, you're in shock and you're bleeding a lot, don't move." A few other bystanders carried Tatiana and laid her in front of me. "We're going to be ok, help is coming." I said. She looked at me and said, "I'm sorry." Then she began seizing, I cried and screamed, "don't die, please God don't let her die!" Her eyes rolled completely into the back of her head; her body rigid and convulsing. She was all I felt I had. "God don't take her too", I pleaded. Then the ambulances came. God was with us that day. We were really banged up; I still have the scar from the seatbelt burn, but we survived. I didn't speak to her for two months, not until she came to my house crying and apologizing. She begged me to attend her high school graduation, which I did. Nothing was the same. All I could think about was how she betrayed me by sliding in with my aunt's man, causing division in my family, fought my aunt and got us both fired; and that she almost killed me. I spoke to Tatiana one time after that.

I was still riding tough with Tory, but even that went left. I fell real ill and I had to be rushed to the ER. Tory and I had just gotten back from our favorite barbeque spot Everett and Jones. We were on the couch, when this pain shot through me, from my vagina to my stomach. I screamed "Oh my God get off, get off!" I pushed him off me and tried to run to the bathroom, but I was in too much pain and fell to the floor. Still screaming, the pain was getting worse. I had never felt anything like that. I was terrified, and then I began throwing up everywhere. What was going on with me, was it something I ate? I had food poisoning before and this was nothing like it, and food poisoning didn't make my vagina hurt. Was it a bad UTI? I'd never had a

UTI that made me throw up or cause pain like that before. I couldn't stop throwing up, nor could I stop screaming from the pain. Tory gathered my things and carried me to the car. He drove me about 30 minutes away, with me still screaming and vomiting, to the emergency room in Oakland. The doctor did a pelvic exam on me, and had the nurses draw blood and take urine to run some other test. Before my blood and urine results came back, the doctor appeared to know what was going on with me based on the pelvic exam he had done. I will never forget how that doctor yelled at me. He told me that I was throwing my life away. He was being judgmental and presumptuous, but he was right. As I waited for him to come back with my results, I reflected on his words. I really had been throwing my life away up to this point. Yet I covered it up so well. On the outside looking in, I was doing great, especially in the eyes of my peers. I was making money, had two jobs, I was in school. I had, what some considered, a baller boyfriend that wasn't a street dude. In actuality I was still so reckless though. I didn't value my body or my life. The doctor finally came back in and the look on his face was different. He seemed angry and slightly disgusted before, now he seemed somber and concerned. He pulled the stool up in front of me and sat down. He proceeded to tell me that the infection was what he feared it was and that upon my vaginal exam he could see the infection was pretty bad and that this kind of infection can make me sterile. I looked confused, which quickly changed to shock when he said, "Ms. Brown you may never be able to have children." That statement echoed. I felt as if the entire emergency room heard what he just said and heard the loud thud of my heart falling to the floor. An STD?! I had never had one before. I was out there, but I was careful. I trusted Tory and he burned me. Not long after that, he confessed to cheating on me with his ex. That explained why she went off one night when she buzzed to get in the apartment building and I answered the intercom. Then to find out that he went behind my back trying to cheat on me with my best friend, Lynae, after meeting her when she came to visit me. The icing on the cake was to find out he had also had sex with Tatiana, during the time I wasn't speaking to her. Not only did he betray me, but he betrayed his best friend too. It would take several months but I was done. I was breaking up with Tory, until I found out I was pregnant.

I had moved to Vallejo with my grandma and got a full-time job at a dental office there. My life was quiet here, and now was not the time to have a baby, especially with Tory. I made my abortion appointment, and then told him. He tried to change my mind, but I was not hearing it. My mind was made up. Until I started having doubts; could I kill my baby? So, I began praying. Truly praying, which I didn't do much. I was asking God, pleading with Him, that if it wasn't meant to be to take this baby before my appointment. God did just that. The week of my appointment I began passing clots while at work. My good friend there told me to go to the ER. I did, and I found out I was miscarrying. They said the fetus hadn't passed and to keep my abortion appointment to ensure everything is taken out. For two days I was in so much pain; my body felt like it was in the fight of my life. I slept in the living room, so my grandma wouldn't hear my cries, since our rooms were next to each other. That Saturday came, and Tory picked me up and took me to my appointment. I was hoping the clinic would tell me I didn't have to have the procedure done. Part of the fetus was still in there though, but I didn't feel as guilty, because I knew I couldn't save it anyway. I was so relieved; then heartbreak set in. The realization hit me that I had a miscarriage. The doctor was right, I couldn't have children. My body failed me because I failed it. As I sat in that chair with that heating pad on my tummy to help with the cramping and wait for the pain medication to kick in, I drifted into my thoughts. I tuned out the noise of the business lines ringing, and other women sitting around me engaged in conversations about the abortions they had had. How could women do this more than once? I wondered. It was horrible: the sound of the machine as it sucked out what was left inside of me out and how cold that room was, and the smell of blood. The pain it caused physically, and the unexpected emotional pain too. I had a life inside of me, a baby. What if this was the only chance I had, and I had asked God to take it away from me. Would I regret this decision, that prayer, for the rest of my life? I couldn't get my due date out of my head as I sat there, and it made me so sad. As I sat there, I no longer felt the physical pain. All I could feel then was emotional pain. All I could feel now was sad - sad and tired. I was completely drained. I came to the conclusion that I had to put my brave face back on and be at peace with this. At breakfast afterwards, Tory was so crushed. I was at peace though and didn't let him bring me down with him. I cut things off with him and went my separate way. It was time for some changes in my life.

## 15: COULD THIS BE LOVE

Since I was single and staying home more, I had more time to spend with my grandma. She asked me if I would like to visit some churches with her. I figured why not, since the last church I had attended was my great-uncle's church in Watts when I was about eleven years old. We visited several churches over the course of a couple of months. One in particular was a tiny church. It reminded me of the church at the end of the movie "A Color Purple." It was small and white, with wooden pews. The sound of tambourines, an organ, and drums filled this small space. There weren't very many people there, but the presence I felt made the church seem so full. I felt a sense of safety there, unlike at the other churches we visited. Yet, I knew that sense of safety from somewhere. It was the same safety I had felt when I would hold my Bible close to me when I was younger. There was a pureness here that I hadn't experienced before. I don't remember what the sermon was about, but the preacher preached it with such passion. He was shouting and sweating, and speaking in a language unknown to me. Some of the other people in the pews spoke in this unfamiliar language too. Oddly, it didn't throw me off; I was so into the service. I was so captivated by the energy there. They called for those needing prayer and my grandma asked me if I wanted to go. I wasn't too familiar with someone praying for me, or even me praying for myself. I mean, I had brief conversations with God from time to time. Mostly along the lines of: "God please help me", but what did I have to lose now? As I walked to the front, I began thinking about what I would want them to pray for. Would I ask them, or would they ask me? I noticed people falling down around me and I got scared. I thought about turning around to go back to my seat. I turned my head and saw my grandma waving me to keep walking. I came to a stop at this older dark-skinned woman. She didn't ask me anything and I didn't tell her anything, but she prayed and spoke about the things I thought were secret. How did she know these things? Was she a psychic? What kind of church was this? She then put one hand on my belly and another on my lower back and began speaking in that language and out of nowhere tears began falling from my eyes. Weights felt like they were lifting off me. My stomach got hot, and then a burning sensation filled my entire body. What was happening to me? I cried harder; afraid yet comforted. After that day, I wanted to know more about God. I wanted to go to church all the time. I wanted to actually read my Bible and not just keep it near me to feel safe in times of trouble. My grandma and I didn't join that church, but we did join one in Vallejo. I began attending church regularly. Things were changing, and they seemed to be for the better; a new job, another city, and all my troubles were behind me.

My good friend at work decided after some time that she wanted to introduce me to a good family friend of theirs, named Marshall. He was in the Air Force. She brought a picture of him to work; I took one look and literally said, "That's going to be my husband!"

From pretty much the beginning, this relationship was dysfunctional, but nobody could tell me this wasn't love. Life seemed so slow and normal with him though. A normalcy I craved so desperately, or was it? How normal could it possibly be between two damaged souls coming together, relying on our relationship to mend everything our lives had broken in us?

He was so possessive and jealous, and I was so needy. One night while sleeping in his dorm, I was awakened by my ankle being yanked and my head hitting the wooden bed frame and then the floor. It took me a minute to get my bearings before I could hear him yelling at me to get out. He was throwing my clothes all over the room, calling me a hoe and yelling at me about disrespecting him. I was confused; what was he talking about and why was he talking to me like this? Everything was fine when I fell asleep. He walked over to his computer and turned it on and my email messages popped up on the screen. How did he get into my email account? I hadn't given him the password. He told me he looked over my shoulder while I was logging in and memorized the password; I was floored, but still confused because I hadn't done anything. He opened a message from my ex-boyfriend, JD, that read:

"Shawnetta,

I know you have a man now, so this isn't that type of message. I just wanted to tell that I'm sorry for anything I've done to hurt you. He is lucky to have you and I wish you the best.

Love always, JD"

Why was he so mad? I didn't do anything, and neither did my ex. Yet, here I was crying my eyes out and feeling so guilty. This was the dynamic of our relationship though; Marshall's jealous rages and rants made me feel needed and wanted. This was how it was supposed to be, right? If he didn't love me then he wouldn't care, right? My grandma and my aunt tried repeatedly to warn me about how unhealthy our relationship was and how bad he was for me. My grandma warned that a relationship that begins with those types of issues only progresses to worse; could even become abusive. They were wrong about him though, because nobody is that concerned with you unless they truly love you. Love, real love, hurts sometimes, right? I saw it with my own eyes with mom and daddy. They were still married, so something must be right.

September 11, 2001. My phone rang, it was him "Babe you can't leave the room today. The base is on lockdown." I didn't understand; I thought maybe another retiree got caught shoplifting, but he sounded so terrified. "Why? Why do you sound like that?" I asked. He told me to turn on the news. I couldn't believe what I was seeing and hearing. I cried all day, because to witness such evil was so devastating and terrifying. He was on edge after that; he knew he was going to have to go to war. We fought so much after that; he was taking all of his fear and stress out on me. He then got his orders, just as we suspected. He was off to Khandahar, Afghanistan. We had a huge fight and broke up over the phone before he even made it there. Single and free, I was back to my old ways. After only a month we got back together. I needed him, and he made me feel like he needed me; that made me feel so complete. While he was gone, I found out that he wasn't as loyal as I had thought; another man betraying me, story of my life. I would find letters when I checked the mail; messages when I cleared the voicemail; numbers on the back of receipts when I cleaned his room for inspection. Right back into depression I slipped. All I did was work, take care of his affairs on base, stayed at home, and argue with Marshall - either on the phone on in the letters we wrote one another.

Prior to Marshall returning home, we briefly broke up again and I found myself in the arms of JD. Only this time something new had developed; JD and I became intimate, sealing what appeared to be the hold he had on my soul.

Marshall got his orders, he was coming back home, and he promised me that we were going to get married. My focus was back on him. We were working things out and he wanted me to be his wife. For me, that was the ultimate honor. He came home, and we got our place, but no wedding date. Nothing changed. Instead, things got worse because now we lived together. All the fighting seemed to be endless. I was never good enough; I was always feeling guilty about things I shouldn't. The manipulation and verbal abuse was horrible. He wasn't putting his hands on me, but he might as well have. His words were slowly destroying me. I was reliving my youth, except now, I was someone I said I'd never be: I was my mom.

I decided I was done, and I was moving out. I had moved a few things back into my grandma's house, only to move them right back into our apartment. I was pregnant. I didn't want my child to be a statistic. I was given another shot at this, so I was keeping my baby. If Marshall didn't run when I told him that I was pregnant, then I wouldn't run from him. He didn't run and together we stayed. He got out of the military while I was pregnant. We fought so much about that too, and I was also fighting so much with my mom during this time. I began to reject him; which only made things worse, if that were even possible. I was so hurt, damaged, and I didn't trust him. He would get off work and not come home for hours. He wouldn't answer his phone or return my calls. He was cheating while I was carrying his child. I couldn't prove it, but my intuition wasn't lying to me; neither was his demeanor, or the fact that he was coming home all hours of the night.

It was such a stressful pregnancy. When I finally laid eyes on my baby boy, the tears just flowed. After thirty-seven hours of hard labor and an emergency cesarean section, my perfect baby boy was here! For the second time in my life I saw my face looking back at me. The doctor said I would not be able to have children, yet here was this beautiful baby boy: my miracle. I was overcome with a love like I'd never felt before; a love I didn't know I was capable of; a love I didn't think I deserved to feel. I was also terrified because he was a boy. So far, most of the males in my life had done nothing but hurt and betray me in some kind of way. The only two that didn't was my grandpa Bo and my grandpa John. Would this child betray me? I loved him too much to care though. Would I be good enough for him? Would I be a better mom than what I felt I had had? I didn't know, but I knew I would give my life to be the best for him.

## 16: WHY DID I COME BACK

When my son was just two months old, Marshall convinced me to move back to the Antelope Valley: the city that was filled with so much hurt from my most terrifying years. I was back there and I didn't want to be. True to form, hurt, chaos, betrayal, depression, loss, and defeats, all met me here in this city. Now our fights were becoming physical; more manipulation and hurt. Marshall said I wouldn't have to work, and I could just finish school, but within a month he was calling me lazy and worthless. He was stressing over bills, but this was his idea. I was holding up to my end of the deal. It was still never good enough.

I ended up quitting school and getting a job at a local dental office. The manipulation and hurt didn't just come from him, but my mom and daddy too. Daddy was still intimidating me, and was verbally and mentally abusive in so many ways. I was an adult, a mother myself, and practically a wife, yet daddy still had so much control over me, like when I was child. My mom seemed like she was meaner towards me. She was almost always agitated with me and I didn't know why.

It would take me years to find out the things she struggled with and about the demons she battled that had taken such a tremendous toll on her. I just figured she'd been in her abusive marriage for so long that she was successfully coping. I had no clue that all that my mom was battling ran as deep as it did. The truth about what she had endured and why she had endured it was far uglier than I could ever imagine. I hadn't figured it out at this point, so I took it as her mirroring daddy's abusive ways. One morning, while temporarily working with my mom to make more money, she called me to come down to the parking lot and help her bring up her coffee. When I made it downstairs, she was furious; she had spilled the coffee in her brand new car. She began yelling at me about coming when she asked. I explained that I had had a call and that I came as soon as I could. The things she was saying and the tone in which she was talking to me was too familiar, and were cutting me so deep. Every word was razor sharp and hurtful. She handed me the coffee, still yelling at me. I had had enough. I took the coffee and looked at her as I fought back tears and yelled, "Whatever you're mad at I didn't do it. I wasn't even in the car with you." and I walked away. She came running after me screaming and cursing even more and yanked me by my hair and began slapping and punching me. I completely forgot who she was, and who I was to her. I forgot where we were, and I went into total defense mode. I fought my mom in that parking lot; releasing hurt with every punch I hit her with. I didn't have much self-control, but just enough to keep me from completely losing it. A close family friend, who also worked with us, broke up the fight. I couldn't believe what had just happened. Then, true to form, I was in the wrong and I took the blame from my family. Her actions were justified, simply because she was the mom. Why did they always make excuses for her? Why was I always expected to be the bigger person? She's the mom, it should be her. This dynamic was wearing me down. I'd rather not have a mom; at this point, I was feeling like I didn't have much of one anyway. I ended up quitting that job, even though I really needed it. I joined a local church that would completely change my life - not before I turned back to my drugs of choice: men and alcohol.

I began cheating. I was tired of Marshall's indiscretions and lies. He was entertaining women on phone chat lines, cyber chat rooms, and taunting me with all of it. He'd leave the house and tell me how he was going to meet up with other women, since I was intimate with him enough. I couldn't be, because the way he treated me didn't make me feel sexy. The names he called me and the things he said to me, didn't make me feel beautiful. When I was intimate with him I felt like I was some random loose woman off the street. The hurtful things he'd say to me, and the memories of the terrible arguments would just play in my head the entire time.

I was also tired of the strained relationship with mom and how it was causing a strain on my relationship with other family members. I felt like my world was caving in around me. I needed my fix; I needed to numb myself. I needed revenge to hurt Marshall the way he hurt me. So I decided to give him a taste of his own medicine, and fed my addiction at the same time. I started with JD; I knew that would hurt him the most. The grasp that I had forgotten he had on my soul, became tighter. I couldn't shake it, or him. I loved my Marshall though; I didn't want to destroy my relationship, I just wanted to hurt him the way he hurt me. My plan back-fired and it tore me up inside; the pain I intended for Marshall inflicted me instead. In the midst of it all, I received a voicemail from my grandpa Bo while I was at work. He had just spent the weekend with us, shopping for a big boy bed for my son. He was just calling to tell me that he loved and enjoyed the time he spent with us. That would be the very last time I would ever hear his voice. Before I finished my shift, he was gone and I had no clue. I didn't even know he had been so sick – it was hidden from me. The doctor had given him a year to live, and that year was up. His body was tired, his heart couldn't take anymore, and neither could mine. I remember crying on my living room sofa that night with Lynae right by my side. I seemed to cry for hours upon hours that night and Marshall was not very comforting. I was hurt from the pain of losing my Grandpa and the disappointment of feeling as if Marshall wasn't there for me. Even with Lynae by my side, I still felt abandoned and alone. Grandpa Bo was the toughest loss for me up until that point in my life. I cried for weeks and kept replaying that voicemail. I wasn't ready to let him go; I needed more time. I clung on to every memory of him as if it were my last breath:

the smell of his favorite cigar mixed with his Old Spice cologne; the memory of him greeting us with the biggest hugs, and introducing us to all the workers at the car wash he managed. One of the only two men to never hurt, betray, disappoint, or violate, me in any way. I wasn't a daddy's girl, daddy hated me. My biological father was locked up and never really knew me. I was grandpa Bo's little girl though.

Not long after my grandpa's memorial service, my boyfriend moved out, and I was alone. JD stopped answering my calls – once again, not there when I needed him. I hated myself, and I was suicidal again. Six months later, Marshall and I attempted to lay everything out on the table. We promised to start off with a clean slate and forgive one another. It was an extremely rough time. I quickly regretted confessing anything to him. It was always about what I did and never what he did. The little respect Marshall had for me went out the window. The verbal abuse only got worse, much worse. Even though we shouldn't have, we finally married. Now I was his wife, his property, and because he hadn't truly forgiven me I became his prey.

## 17: WHY DID I GET MARRIED

Marshall had so much hatred in his heart for me, and he didn't have any problem letting me know it. He preyed on my every weakness, my guilt, shame, and the fact that I needed to be forgiven by him. My name was no longer Shawnetta. I was now the all too familiar, bitch, slut, and whore. I didn't hear "I love you" but instead "I hate you!" I began having anxiety attacks and it felt like I was having a heart attack each time. One was so bad that I was hospitalized. I woke from a terrible nightmare in tears and I couldn't breathe. In my dream Marshall had taken our son, and left me for another woman. They were taunting me. Tormenting me with all the demons I struggled with. They were taunting me with my fears of being a bad mom, having a failed marriage, being unloved; becoming my mom. I couldn't see the woman's face, but her complexion and hair were so clear. It seemed so real, I literally felt heartbreak and devastation. I was so desperate and begging him to stay. Reaching out to touch him and our son, but they wouldn't let me close enough. The woman just kept laughing at me; an evil laugh. She had taken them from me and I had nothing left. I sat up on the edge of the bed and called out to him to take me to call 911. Marshall wouldn't even call an ambulance for me. He was so unaffected by what was happening with me, and watched me struggle to breathe. He only took me in when I tried to call my mom. He didn't want anyone to see him treat me the way he did. None of his friends, very few of mine, and neither of our families. The way he treated me was, for the most part, for our eyes only. That was exactly what I had witnessed growing up. I had married daddy and I became my mother. Once I had gotten to the emergency room, various test were ran on me. My heart was no longer beating, it was fluttering. I was diagnosed with Atrial Fibrilation and hospitalized until my heart beat regulated. That was a result of the stress my marriage had on me. I had to be on blood pressure medication, and baby aspirin for a year after that. Why wasn't that still not enough to make me leave? Only difference was nobody was being molested or violated. I was literally choked though and threatened by Marshall; daddy choked me too. Marshall verbally and emotionally abused me; daddy did too. I was even drug by my arm across the floor of a club by

Marshall; daddy had drug me multiple times before as well. It was so ugly and tumultuous, and I even became quite abusive myself. Like my mother though, I took pride in "being married." This kind of love - ugly love - was all I knew. I had no other example to follow. I was trying and fighting so hard to save my crumbling marriage. I felt like a failure. During this time is when I said yes to God for the first time. If I thought hell was breaking out in my life before, I was really in for a raging storm now.

During that time, I joined the Praise Dance Ministry at my church. I had been a member there for three years and wasn't active in ministry at all. It was time for me to get more involved, plus I needed something to keep me from reverting back to my old ways. Dancing was a love of mine, and something I did so well. To discover that I could still dance and serve God was awesome and life-changing for me. Our group was named G.U.I.Dance (God U and I Dance). It was comprised of six women and one young man. All from various walks of life and with different testimonies. Yet, we all bonded in the most special way. I began to dance through all my pain and struggles. As our dance leader would say, I began to minister through it. Even though I had so much support from that group, my personal life was becoming too much for me to cope with.

I literally almost lost my mind and it landed me in jail twice. The first time was when I found out from our son that my husband had been getting acquainted with a teacher from our son's preschool. Marshall had allowed both her and her son to stay the night with him and our son. We were living separately, but were still supposed to be trying to work things out, so, naturally, this upset and hurt me. I called the school, thinking that because this was a Christian school, I expected them to do something about their employee's inappropriate dealings with my husband. The administrator agreed with me and set up a conference with all three of us. The way my husband treated me in that meeting, in front of them, was so humiliating and devastating. Leaving there, I felt a shift in me and it wasn't good. I called my mom and then my praise dance leader to pray with me. It didn't really help; I was too far gone at that point. I walked to his car, keys in hand, and scratched every ounce of pain into that shiny black paint. He came out of the school to find me keying his car and started yelling and cussing at me. He tried to wrestle the keys out of my hand and we began fighting; both of us swinging and punching. I was pulling his hair, scratching his face, and pulling his shirt so hard the collar ripped. He called the police on me, once he was finally free from my grip. I sat on the step and waited for the officers and just cried. When they came they spoke to him, and tried speaking to me. All I could do was cry and wonder if my son witnessed that horrific display. I had become so angry with him, and resorted to the only way I knew how to express and defend myself. It's what I had learned seeing my mom and daddy. It was what had developed in my own relationship with him: violence. The officer asked if I wanted them to take him, but let me know they had to take me due to the visible marks on my husband. After all of this, I still didn't want him in trouble. I didn't want to risk his job as a fireman, or risk our son not having either one of us. I still was more concerned about him and our son than I was about myself. I still loved him, more than I loved myself. Through my tears, I whispered "no" and the officer cuffed me and led me to his patrol vehicle. My cell phone rang and the officer answered it; he didn't have to, but he felt sorry for me. It was my mom, I could hear her voice. He didn't let me talk to her, but he told her I was being arrested.

As I sat in a jail cell for the first time, all I did was talk to God. I literally prayed and praise danced my way through those three days in jail; playing in my head songs I ministered to; dancing out the choreography took me out of that tiny cell. I was in church on the green carpeted pulpit, looking out at the faces of the congregation that filled the padded green seats. I was up there with my sisters and brother in ministry. I could hear my pastor's voice rooting us on. I didn't eat, and I barely slept. My husband never came for me. Instead, Marshall had me served me with court papers while in that cell. I was in there for felony domestic violence and felony vandalism charges; me, a woman who had had only one traffic violation in her life, facing two felony charges. I had done a lot of dirt, but had never been caught for it, and now here I was in jail looking at being a felon. How did it come to this and why did I let it? What would happen to me now, and my son? Would he lose his mommy? Would I lose my son? Monday came, and it was a long day. We, other inmates and I, waited in that cell to see the judge and learn our fate. Each person that went before the judge, ended up being held and transferred to county jail. I got more and more terrified with each lady that didn't return to that cell. I kept trying to call my husband, but he wouldn't accept my calls. Out of everyone I could've called, I wanted him. I needed him. Plus, I had just started my new job working for a reputable hospital, and now I might lose that job and end up on this bus to county with the rest of these women. It was down to the last two: me and one other. Then a Sheriff came in and called my name, but he had come in from a different door than they had been calling from all day. My heart raced; I thought I was going to faint. I walked over to him and he led me into this small area with two desks and another deputy. He handed me a form to sign, and then a couple of other documents. He took a deep sigh and looked at me, "You are one very lucky woman today, and you have some angels looking out for you", he said. It still didn't register what was going on. "You're free to go, and don't come back here, this isn't the place for you", he continued. He led me out another door and there was my mom, three of my friends from church, and an attorney from my mom's job. They all came to represent and support me; they were also expecting I'd be going before the judge that days. I cried so hard; it was truly a miracle. I didn't see a judge or the inside of that courtroom at all. In spite of my husband wanting to press charges, all charges were dropped by the District Attorney's office. All I had to do was pay about two hundred dollars for the damage to my husband's car. God heard my prayers, again!

I ended up back with my husband because he wanted to work things out, but things were no better. I was having dreams and visions during this time. I had always had them periodically, but now more than I ever had before: things about the future. Most of it was scaring me, or was it preparing me? I was praying to God to show me, to send a sign that I could not mistake. Then one day while I was sitting on my bed, my husband got upset with me, yelling about how much I disgusted him and how much he hated me. Then he literally spit in my face; the lowest of the low. Talk about a sign, right? So then why did I still stay? Six months later I would find myself back in handcuffs again. This time I would end up with a non-violent misdemeanor infraction, but because of my prior arrest I was placed on summary probation and ordered into anger management for twelve months. How did I keep letting him bait me the way he did? He had so much control over me, and I always let him off the hook with everything. I was always the one to forgive, but never the one forgiven. He said he wanted a divorce, but he was sending so many mixed signals. I'd fall for them every time, holding onto hope that I could save my marriage. One day he still loved me, then the next he hated me. Every time I fell for the things he'd say and do, I'd be blindsided by more hurt and betrayal. Did he really want to divorce me, or did he just want me to suffer for all the pain I've caused him? Why couldn't he forgive me the way I had forgiven him? Then the ultimate betrayal; an attack I never saw coming.

He filed a restraining order, which we both had done multiple times. This one was different though, the things stated in that paperwork weren't true and he was asking for sole custody of our son. As shocked as I was, I wasn't worried because I just knew that I was a great mom. No judge would agree to this. During the hearing though the judge did agree and ordered him sole custody and me supervised visitation. I couldn't believe what I was hearing. I never had him arrested; I actually protected him from being arrested and he does this? I never attacked him as a father. I never tried to take our son from him. Did he really hate me that much to come in here and lie to the judge like that? I have seen drug addicts and criminals that hadn't lost custody of their children. Here I was, an upstanding citizen, with a good job, and I really was an amazing mother. I loved my son and provided for him; I protected him. I had never done anything to harm my son. Yet, I was the one on supervised visitation. I had just lost custody of my son, and it'd be an entire year before we would go before the judge to revisit that order. I was devastated. As I walked out of the courtroom, I collapsed. I hit the concrete and just cried. There was so much pain; like my heart had just been ripped right out of my chest. One of my very dear friends, Asha, was there with me. She picked me up off the concrete and walked me out of the courthouse. When we got outside we were met with the sight of my husband driving off leaving two laundry baskets of my belongings on the curb. Such humiliation and sense of betrayal I had felt while having these strangers walking past me and looking at me as we lugged these laundry baskets to my car. Then my car wouldn't start. My battery had died; out of habit, I called him. I was so angry with myself; I had become my mom; so weak and defeated. He threw me away and here I was still holding on. I couldn't lean on my family; they seemed to not want to anger the beast in the fear that he would keep my son from them. Nobody spoke up for me; nobody came to my defense during this time. He could do, and did, whatever he wanted because he knew that nobody had my back. Still, I fought for my marriage, for my family.

Only by now I was no longer just fighting him, he wasn't fighting alone anymore. The terrible nightmare that previously sent me to the hospital, was now my reality- right down to the complexion and hair color that was so clear. Marshall had someone, another obstacle that threatened my ability to hold onto what was rightfully mine. I had to fight against a woman that didn't care that I was his wife and mother of his child; someone that didn't care that Marshall and my son were all I had; someone that didn't value my family and marriage the way I did; someone that used my failures to attack me as a wife and mother. I wasn't the perfect wife, and maybe I didn't love him like he needed, but I didn't really know how. Still, I was the best wife I knew to be, and was an amazing mother. I wasn't about to lose all I had without a fight. So, I continued to fight hard, but I was losing miserably. Then I just gave up, and tried to move on as best as I could. I tried to come to terms with the fact that my marriage was over. Just like in my dream, Marshall had left me for someone else. Although I still had hope, I had no fight left. I just wanted this all to be over. My church and my praise dance ministry at church was what kept me going. My pastor was the only person, out of all my family and friends that wrote a character affidavit for me to take to court. Everyone else refused. When I had needed a place to stay, I asked my mom and she told me to ask daddy. He told me "Hell no!" I had nobody. Hazel didn't have room in her house, or she would have. I began to lean on a familiar person from my past. JD still had my soul in his grasp. It was the comfort of someone familiar, yet the safety of not being hurt because I knew what to expect from him. I was now accustomed to our arrangement. I expected nothing outside of what I was given, and I was satisfied with that. Being at the mercy of JD's convenience was better than nothing at all. It wasn't about the sex though; it really wasn't ever about the sex with anyone I'd been with. For me it was the connection and attention, whenever available, that I was addicted to; that false sense of love and belonging. It's the typical void that any woman with daddy issues has and feels; that deep, dark, big, black, bottomless pit. JD had always been good at filling, or appearing to fill, this void in my life. A role he played very well since I was sixteen years old. This time was no different between us. Guilt consumed me though. What I was doing was so wrong because I was still married. I still wanted my husband, though he gave up on and abandoned me; I still wanted our family. Marshall sensed it, no matter how I tried to mask it. He played on that, and began to give me more false hope. He began, again, to make me think that I would get all that I was losing back. I believed all the signals he was sending my way. I clung to every word and hint of hope, even though he had someone else. That was a period of a lot of confusion for me. I was so angry with him, but I felt no better than him since I had JD around. No better than Marshall and who he was with. Marshall was still my husband and I believed God would spare my marriage. My faith in that, would be the reason I was back in the fight again. Only I was fighting in vain. I was growing weary and defeated. Then one day, at the advice of someone from church, I began praying to be free. I prayed to God to take away any love I had for Marshall. With tears in my eyes, I prayed for the strength and courage to let him go. I begged God for the ability to stand on my own without him. I asked God to cover our son and to shield him from all the ugliness that was his mother and father's marriage. I didn't want our son to be disappointed in either one of us. At that moment, I needed all of that, more than I needed my marriage.

Over the course of my divorce and custody battle, I got evicted twice and had two cars repossessed. Sometimes I didn't even have hot water because I spent bill money on attorney and court fees. I would lie to my son and tell him the shower was broken so he wouldn't tell his dad. I was fighting to get my son back; which eventually I did. My divorce was finalized after almost three years of fighting. God was right there in the courtroom. It was as if every loss I had faced in that courtroom in all that time had been erased. I didn't have to fight dirty like he was fighting. I didn't have to lie or manipulate. I leaned on God and He showed up and showed completely out. We had the same judge the entire process. On that final day when we showed up, it was a new judge and he dismissed everything that had been against me from all the previous hearings. He even stated that I should've never lost custody or been ordered to supervised visitation. I couldn't believe my ears. I cried, but this time tears of joy. God had not forgotten me, He heard my prayers, and now victory was mine. I got everything I asked for in my divorce – including being freed of any romantic or loving feelings towards Marshall. He hated me even more for it. Years of chaos followed from that situation, but by the grace of God, my son held up very well; he always managed to be so strong and at times even strengthened me.

## 18: BE STILL AND KNOW THAT I AM GOD

I was living with my friend Tay. Two single moms and two boys. Tay became like a sister, and we became a family. It was during this time that I discovered me, the real me. I learned to love me, forgive me, and see myself how God sees me. While God was working on me, I had no clue that He was also preparing me for someone. I met my second husband, Virgil, during this time. He joined the dance ministry at church, and we became friends. Unexpectedly, things just took off from there. It was like a fairytale. He held me up in so many ways, and loved me in a way I had never experienced before. He even prayed over me while I slept. Virgil just had to be sent to me from God. What I had with him was everything I prayed for. I completely surrendered all of myself to this man. This was the first time ever that I didn't feel the need to be guarded. I displayed a transparency that I almost couldn't control. It was as if God wouldn't allow me to block anything He was doing with Virgil and I. Virgil was the first person I told, in whole, about what daddy had done to me. I told Marshall a small portion of it early in our relationship.

The way Marshall reacted to what I had shared with him brought me shame. After that I never spoke on it, to anyone else, until the day I told Virgil. He made me feel so safe letting him into the darkest places of my heart. He encouraged me and gave me the strength to tell my mom.

When I did, I got the feeling she already knew. If she didn't know everything, she certainly already knew more than I believed she did. She didn't leave daddy, which I expected and hoped for. I wanted so badly for her to choose me; but she went on with things as usual though, and even kept referring to him as my dad. I was so hurt by that. She is my mother; how can she even stand to be with him or near him knowing what he did? Being a mother, myself, I couldn't understand her ability to go on on as she did; knowing what she knew. I loved my mom, she was the only one I had, but I began to distrust her. Not only around myself, but also around my son. In my mind, if she was ok with what daddy had done, then she had to be a guilty party in it as well. After revealing my truth about what I had endured my brother turned his back on me. He felt he had to choose a side, and he chose his father's. Why was this monster always chosen over me by the people I loved the most?

One night, my mom invited me to dinner to talk. As I sat across the table from her expressing how I was feeling about everything, she looked me in my face and told me, "If I tell you how I really feel about it, you and I will probably never speak again." It was as if she was telling me she didn't care, or she didn't believe me. I was so hurt by her and I had to come to terms with the fact that she will always choose him over me. Maybe she was like that because of her own life experiences. Was she really a bad mom, or was it that her best wasn't good enough for me because I could never see myself being that way with my son. I not only expected, but I needed so much from her as a mother. By that point it seems like I was fighting a losing battle. Whatever it was, I had to press on. I cut off all communication daddy had with myself and my son. When I distanced myself from him, some of his side of the family distanced themselves from me. I began to doubt how I really felt. Was I being ungrateful towards the man that took on the responsibility of raising a child that wasn't his? Did I owe him more gratitude and respect for keeping a roof over my head, and clothes on my back? I was disgusted with myself for thinking that way. The things he had done to me, no child should endure. He had done some good, but it was far outweighed by the bad. I was right to feel that he was a monster. I called him daddy, but he had never really been a daddy to me. That would be the time in my life that I would come to realize that I was fatherless. I tried to move forward with my life; hurt and all, and I just kept going.

I started seeing a therapist again, and was diagnosed with PTSD and Anxiety disorder from all the abuse I endured. I was surprised. Even though I lived it, I hadn't realized just how traumatic my life had been up to that point. During that time, my biological father was looking for me. His wife had found my old Myspace account and messaged me. We began writing letters and I allowed him to call me - he was still in prison. Communication with him confirmed some vague memories; memories of molestation that weren't tied to daddy, but took place when I was around infant to toddler age. He also revealed to me that his mother molested him and his brothers. This spirit of perversion was heavy in my family for generations. God used me to break the cycle. Now that the cycle was broken, I realized that I wasn't ready to have a relationship with him. What he did, wouldn't allow me to have him near me or my son when he got out of prison. He represented the monster in my life, and since I hadn't forgiven him at that point, I couldn't forgive my biological father either. So I changed my number and stopped responding to his letters.

Things were going well with Virgil. I was happy. I was healing, and working on my forgiveness. We got married after only ten months of dating. It seemed quick, but it felt so right. My son adored him, and had already established a strong bond with him. It was as though God had answered my prayers down to the smallest detail concerning this relationship.I was living my happily ever after.

Seven months into the marriage I found out I was pregnant. I was on cloud nine! I never imagined my life being like this. When I was nineteen, the doctor told me I wouldn't have any children. For several years, my life appeared to be evidence that I wouldn't find love again, let alone get pregnant again. Yet, here I was happily married, with custody of my son, and now expecting another baby. My heart was so full; I felt so blessed.

Then a month after finding out I was pregnant, a bomb dropped. On July 4, 2012 my husband confessed to cheating. While driving to a friend's house to celebrate the holiday, he tearfully confessed. I had no clue; how could I have not known? Was he that good, or was I that naïve? He'd been cheating from the very beginning of our relationship. I felt like everything up to that point was a complete lie. Why wouldn't God just allow me happiness? I even found messages between him and one of my friends from church. She was in the dance ministry with us, and serving alongside us. She was on fire for the Lord just like us. We shared a love for music, fashion, food, ministry, and a deep love for the things of God. Unbeknownst to me, we were sharing my husband too. For two months they lied to me about things. For two months I had vivid dreams showing me everything. Why wouldn't they just tell the whole truth? I saw the messages, and now God was revealing the truth to me in my dreams. I was tormented; I couldn't sleep. Week after week, rehearsal after rehearsal, meeting after meeting, and Sunday after

Sunday, I had to pull the truth out of them one detail at a time. It was pure torture; finally, the entire truth, or as much of it as I would ever get, came out. She had slept with my husband multiple times, even in our home in our bed while I was at work. Even though she wasn't the only one, that infidelity hurt me the most. I was so betrayed, so hurt. I trusted her, I trusted him. We were in ministry together. Didn't that mean anything to them. This never happened to me when I was in the world; how could they do this? How could this happen not only in my home, but in my church home? This church was my "safe place" and now my church no longer felt safe. Again, nobody fought for me and nobody really spoke up for me. I wanted my church family to be just as angry and outraged as I was. Yet, nobody really seemed angry with them, or disappointed in them; instead they appeared to receive pity and love – as if they were the victims. I felt as if nobody wanted to touch this situation. Nobody wanted to be responsible for handling it, or maybe nobody knew how to handle it. I didn't know who I could trust or turn to. I felt like I was fighting through that all by myself. I truly felt betrayed by my husband, her, and my church. Talk about church hurt! God used that situation to show me the imperfect side of the people of God. I had placed Christians on such a high and unrealistic pedestal, and as I related to them, had placed myself up there too. That was a tough, yet humbling, lesson for me. I pressed through, still attending church and operating in ministry with them; painfully refusing to quit.

I was always on edge at work, and when I would come home, I would walk through my house inspecting every little thing that seemed off. As if one thing out of place would uncover the truth about more of my husband's indiscretions. Consumed with thoughts, questions, and visions, my insecurities began controlling me. Was I not beautiful enough? Was my body night nice enough? Was I a bad lover or a bad wife? What was it that they, these women, had that I didn't? What did she have that was so amazing that my husband was willing to jeopardize, not only his marriage and family, but his ministry too? My thoughts never turned off, they just kept haunting me. I was so stressed mentally and afraid: afraid of him leaving me for someone else like my Marshall had; terrified of the thought of having to go through another divorce. I couldn't bear the possibility of another custody battle. I even contemplated abortion because I just couldn't go through any of that again. Not with two children. I was even afraid of going back to my old ways. That hurt triggered that urge and my husband was still giving into urges of his own. He didn't even know what caused him to cheat the way he did, or why he had never been monogamous with anyone. This left me feeling like no matter what I did, I couldn't keep him from cheating on me, because I wasn't the reason he did it in the first place. How long could I go through this, and why would God want me to? I wanted to cheat too, make him feel how I was feeling. I tried leaning again on that familiar grasp. JD was back he had never really left. Almost twenty years of the same thing. He always remained within close enough reach. Close enough to make more promises he didn't intend to keep, profess more love, and say everything I needed to hear. JD was telling me everything that my husband wasn't. He remained in close enough reach for me to fall for all of it, every time. I needed him to heal me where my husband wouldn't though. I struggled between what I thought I needed to do, and what God was telling me that He wanted me to do. No matter how much I was tempted, I couldn't bring myself to make the same mistakes that I seemed to have kept making before. I needed God to release my soul from that JD's hold. I was having thought of leaving my husband, but I couldn't do that either - because the harsh reality that I ultimately gave up on my first marriage still haunted me. I questioned whether, or not, I fought hard enough, and long enough. Did I hang in there when Marshall gave up? Did I pray enough when he wouldn't? Was I spiritually strong enough, when he wasn't? The one that struck me to the core was, did I forgive myself when Marshall didn't forgive me? Did I let go out of guilt?

God gave me another chance with Virgil, and even though I wasn't totally convinced that he loved me. I knew that I truly loved him, and I wasn't ready to lose him; I had to fight that fight again. This time I had to fight harder, longer, and smarter. I fought, but I struggled. I just couldn't seem to give it my all. I needed to get away for a while.

I used this opportunity to separate myself from my husband, my church, and this city that held so much of my pain. I went back home for a few days. There's nothing like a peaceful train ride to make things better. I have always had a strong love for trains that began when I was very young. My grandma worked on Amtrak trains and she would bring me with her traveling from state to state, city to city. There was something about the bustle of the passengers as they boarded the train and found their seats; the smell of the coffee coming from the dining car; the vibration of the train as it glided across the tracks, and my grandma coming to check on me "how's my baby girl?" It all was so comforting to me, and no matter how old I got, a nice train ride never lost its touch with me.

God dealt with me so much concerning my marriage, but more so concerning my trust in Him: concerning my yes to Him. Little did I know that when I was praying for the ability to forgive in the situation with Marshall and daddy, that God would use my current marriage to test my ability to forgive. This was a season of learning to lean on and rest in God like I had never done before. I had to just allow God to do what He was going to do. The strain still managed to take a toll on my pregnancy and I went into premature labor twice. After thirteen weeks of bed rest, another beautiful baby boy was born. My first son taught me how to love, and now my second son was a reminder that I could still love. Even in the middle of a raging storm, God still saw fit to bless me beyond measure.

## 19: IT'S A NEW SEASON

Virgil and I got through that extremely trying time. It wasn't easy, and it didn't happen overnight. However, we all got through it - as a couple, as a family, and I got through it as a person. After a couple of years of healing, I began praying for everyone that had ever hurt me, and praying for everyone I had ever hurt. Even though I wasn't completely healed, God had me to begin reaching out to various people in my life. I started with the woman from church that had an affair with my husband. In that moment, God showed me just how strong I truly am; how powerful forgiveness, true forgiveness - His forgiveness - can be. This new season I was in also showed me how much stronger I needed to become, because I still couldn't hear daddy's name without cringing. A new victim had come forth accusing daddy, of some of the same violations I had endured at his hands. I blamed myself so much for that, and questioned if there were others that hadn't had the strength to come forth. I told myself I should've never recanted my story when I was eight years old. I told myself I should've told every time he did something to hurt or violate. He could've been stopped had I not been silenced. My entire life I had labeled my mom as weak for not standing up to him. This incident would show me that I shared in many of those same weaknesses with her. As a result of my weakness, someone else was now accusing him. Someone else witnessed the monster we were so conditioned to keeping secret.

I tormented myself with this and became so bitter. I was still so full of unforgiveness; I began to resent my mother and brother even more. I had convinced myself that all three of us failed that victim, and any others there may have been. My relationship with my brother pretty much became non-existent, and extremely strained with my mom. I walked around with the weight of anger and bitterness, reminiscent of my younger years. It took quite a toll on me mentally and physically. All I could do was pray for all of us, even for daddy. Then one day it broke. While praying on my drive home from work, God lead me to call daddy to ask forgiveness for all my unforgiveness. He didn't answer, so I left a message. Afterwards, I cried so hard that I had to pull over to the shoulder on the freeway. I sat there a short while just staring down at my phone in my hand. These weren't tears of sorrow; they were tears of gratitude and release. I was so grateful to God for the work He had done in me. He used me in His Kingdom and loved me in spite of who I had been and what I had done. He showed me that my heart wasn't black and cold. I wasn't miserable or depressed. I was no longer battling perversion, addiction, or suicide. I had custody of my son and we had a roof over our head. We weren't being evicted and my car wasn't being repossessed. I was in my right mind. I discovered what rue joy was, and I possessed it. Above all, I had peace, so much peace. Daddy never called me back, but the fact that I was willing to forgive spoke volumes of how God was using and would continue to use me. I was finally free. I could finally say that I had survived the enemy in the house.

## 20: IT WAS GOD

I have been through so much in my life, yet still not as much as so many of you that are reading this. For most of my life, I felt as though God was punishing me as if He didn't love me; I even at times doubted if He was even there at all. That's exactly how the enemy, the true enemy, wants us to feel about God. Satan doesn't want us to feel like we can't count on God. I am living proof that it is the exact opposite though, because God was always there. Even when I didn't know Him; even when I wouldn't acknowledge Him, He was there. He did love me, so much. He wasn't punishing me, but instead preparing me. Everything I went through, shaped, molded, equipped, and qualified me for where God was calling me, and what He was calling me to do. Like the footprints in the sand, as I stand in my present looking back on my past, I see two sets of footprints. Even when I felt alone, I wasn't alone. The enemy used many different people and situations in my life, including myself, to do what he does best - kill, steal, and destroy. Despite his many efforts to take me out of here, one way or another, God wouldn't let it be so. I not only survived it all, but God gave me the victory. The strength, the will, the drive, the motivation, the determination - none of that was of my own; the losses and the wins; it was all God and all for a divine purpose. I say to the person reading this right now: There's nothing so terrible about anything that has happened to you or anything you've done that God can't and won't still use you. Whatever the devil intends for bad, God will use it for your good. My life, the very thing that has brought me so much pain, now helps people. The things that had me bound are now used to free others. The things that kept me immobile are now the very things that keep me moving. No more lasting shame, guilt, or pain. Now I am walking in my deliverance, healing, God-given purpose, and I am free to be excited about what the future holds; and so can you!

The following are available public resources for anyone in need:

National Suicide Hotline: (800) 273-8255

National Domestic Violence Hotline: (800) 799-7233

The Childhelp National Child Abuse Hotline: (800) 422-4453

SAMHSA (Substance Abuse and Mental Health Service Administration) National Helpline: (800) 662-4357

Made in the USA
Coppell, TX
24 March 2022